MW00813447

Before she was Mother Goose,
she was just a kid like you.
Cooking meals with mom and dad,
and tasting something new.

Goose Girl learned to rhyme,
and also read and write.
She shared these yummy recipes,
I can't wait to have a bite!

You're learning and you're growing,
with every passing hour.
One day you'll be a Mom or Dad,
and can teach your kids these powers.

- Lacey Mauritz

FOREWORD

It's story time! One of the unique abilities we have as humans to really connect is through the stories we tell. And reading together is one of the earliest activities we can do with children to teach them about our world and beyond. Of course, this cherished together-time with our children typically occurs *sandwiched* in and between meals and snacks, play and chores, school and sports, work and errands, baths, cuddles, sleep and more. But there's no question: Reading together is a vital and life enhancing gift for child and parent alike. Classic nursery rhymes like Mother Goose's are early favorites read again and again, shared from one generation to the next. Why? Because even before they're understood, the sounds of words, alliterations, rhymes, and repetition imprint in the youngest minds, helping them start to discover and understand language. Nursery rhymes are sometimes silly, sometimes bring life lessons—and frequently, a bit of both. And a good number of them—as Lacey discovered with her boys and you soon will too—involve food.

We feed our children from the moment they're born, and in only a few months they begin the process of feeding themselves. It's from that point they start asserting their independence and expressing preferences. This just so happens to be the perfect time to start getting them involved. Once they start picking up objects, even the littlest *little* can help by holding a spoon as they watch you cook or get involved by simply touching—sometimes tasting—the ingredients as they go into a recipe. And their participation advances from there.

Just as reading books aloud together brings a sense of closeness with our children, so does cooking—and playing—with food in the kitchen.

Cooking together can strengthen your emotional bond while you read, talk, measure, and make messes over creating a dish. And that teaches important life lessons about food, mealtime, and nourishment of the body and of the family. Not to mention, it creates memories.

As a doctor of public health, I know there are many factors that make a healthy family and healthy community. Nourishing families physically and emotionally is one of them. And as a fellow dietitian, like Lacey, I know that nutritious meals are a crucial component to overall health, and that at the end of the day, parents want the very best for their family's well-being. Importantly, we also know that most parents want meal planning and prep to be worth the effort, fit their busy, modern lifestyle, and ideally to be pleasurable. This book delivers on all of these.

Cooking with Mother Goose isn't a cookbook simply for parents to help them prepare healthy meals for kids. Nor is it an instructional manual for parents to help teach their children to cook. Instead, it's an adventure in reading classic nursery rhymes through a new lens and bringing them to life by cooking and connecting as a family. Lacey has worked tirelessly, while testing with her own

FOREWORD

family and extended circle of friends and colleagues, to make this cookbook adventure a *fruitful*, fun and flavorful experience for both parent and child. This book provides an activity-based adventure—in both reading and in executing recipes—that's approachable for any parent from the novice in the kitchen to the experienced chef, while including specific tips and helpful explanations on steps your children can assist with or accomplish on their own. And the outcome is again and again: delicious.

Importantly, research shows that kids eat a more varied and balanced diet when they participate in meal preparation. That's quite an amazing bonus you'll find throughout these pages as you and your *littles* experience the fun of reading and preparing delicious recipes together. And while this is not a book specifically about childhood nutrition, you'll get a friendly and welcome dose of that too, woven artfully throughout the pages from an expert mom-dietitian as you explore ingredients, foods, and flavors. But I think the best part—the real gift you'll get from Lacey's book—is all the delicious, family fun you'll have.

Cooking with Mother Goose is personal: You'll feel Lacey's sincerity alongside her expertise, and soon you'll feel she's your confidant and friend as you explore and experiment within every page. She wrote from her head and from her heart. You can't miss her love of family and food. In the early stages of writing, Lacey shared with me that she hoped readers would use this book and write in it, splash on it, earmark pages, and spill tears of laughter (and perhaps also, I mused, from chopping onions) marking the pages with memories. This book is so beautiful with the delightful illustrations, and its gorgeous photography and design that you might be tempted to protect it like you would a special edition. But I encourage you to use it—the greatest compliment you can give a cookbook author—and make it your own. Fill these pages with your experiences and memories as you spend time together in the kitchen.

Each time you open *Cooking with Mother Goose* for either a rhyme or a recipe—or both—you'll be sharing moments that will last a lifetime. You'll foster reading and comprehension, planning and action, collaboration and cooperation, all while learning and practicing important kitchen skills as you share time together—skills that will stay with your children as they grow up into adults and parents themselves someday. Like the marks on the wall charting your children's growth, I have a feeling this book will be with you through every stage of your children's development marking time and experiences. You'll go to bed reading and dreaming of this book of nursery rhymes and tasty recipes... and then wake up with it for breakfast.

I wish you many messy and delicious memories ahead!

Wendy Bazilian, DrPH, MA, RDN

Cooking with MOTHER GOOSE

LACEY J. MAURITZ, RDN

FAMILY-FRIENDLY MEALS

Nursery rhymes and the recipes they inspire from a dedicated mom-dietitian.

TABLE OF CONTENTS

ACKNOWLEDGEMENTS

Thanks to my incredible family and amazing friends! Your encouragement and belief that families need this book gave me the pluck and creativity to make *Cooking with Mother Goose* real.

Of course, I want to thank my boys, Axel and Rex (and you too, Todd). You are the reason behind everything that I do. I love you.

Eleanor and Edward, the world would see an entirely different book had it not been for our friendship! The talent and support of your mum (or Granny as Ed calls her) and the entire family have been incredible. I don't think another grandmother on the planet could create the whimsical, wild and weird drawings for these rhymes. Jacqueline, as they say in Chile, *¡te pasaste!* (You've outdone yourself!)

To my parents, who gave me both the foundation to dream and the support to achieve them, y'all are wonderful. To my in-laws for their unwavering support, you rock!

To my sister and my new niece, baby Hazel, I can't wait to read you rhymes from this book and get into the kitchen together.

To all the recipe contributors, thank you so much for sharing strategies, ideas and recipes so we could make the food in this book the best it could be.

Wendy Bazilian, DrPH, RDN, as dietitians and mothers, we live the reality on these pages! Your mentorship, encouragement and enthusiasm for the health and literacy of young people has given me the courage to share this book with the world.

To my editor, Sarah, and designer, Stockton, I still pinch myself that you agreed to do this project. The coaching, the reading (the re-reading), the designing (and re-designing) and the laughs we had figuring it all out made the process both fun and productive. Sarah, you always advise to "use only the amount of words you need to say what you need to say. No more. No less."

So, in that spirit, to everyone who touched the making of this book and to everyone who picks it up, I say, with exactly the right amount of words,

THANK YOU!

CONTRIBUTORS

AXEL KURZIUS MAURITZ AND REX HARRISON MAURITZ

These littles, my boys, ate every recipe in this book (and taste-tested plenty that didn't make the cut)! I started this project when Axel (on the left) had just turned 4 years old and Rex (on the right) was 2½. Together, they've shown me just what Kids Can do and what Todd and I need to Watch Out For when we are making meals together.

Cooking with Mother Goose is full of their special requests (**Team Chicken Soup, Teriyaki Salmon**) and advice on how to handle the real-life meltdowns over what's for breakfast, lunch and dinner. This dynamic duo has pushed me to put my best food forward. They have inspired me to compile practical, science-based nutritional guidance and share "we-lived-through-this-and-you-will-too" stories. It's thanks to them that this book exists. I couldn't ask for better partners!

To find out more about Axel and Rex, keep in touch with me.
These dudes are too young for social media!

JACQUELINE TAYLOR

Jacqueline (Jaq) is a writer and self-taught artist based out of the UK. She is the loving grandmother of Edward Williams, my son's best friend, and an honorary member of our family. Jaq brought *Cooking with Mother Goose* to life through her art and creativity; I cannot imagine writing this book without her. While Jaq has lent her talents to various private story collections, this book marks the debut of her work to the public.

When Jaq is away from her paints, she spends time outdoors taking satisfaction from the plants and creatures around her. The natural world is her inspiration, from a ladybird landing on her arm to the shade of an oak tree on a summer day.

Find out more about Jacqueline
www.storybooknutrition.com

LORENA SALINAS

Lorena is a professional chef, award-winning blogger and an incredible food photographer. She's the eye behind all of the fabulous photos in this book. Beyond bringing the recipes to life with beautiful visuals, she's helped with the remix of some kid-friendly classics. For recipes we made together, see **Cinnamon Rolls** (p. 171), **Heart Tarts** (p. 153). and **Black and White Pasta Alfredo** (p. 215)

Find out more about Lorena
@cravingsjournal • www.cravingsjournal.com

RACHAEL RYDBECK

Rachael is a Le Cordon Bleu trained culinary instructor with over 15 years experience teaching classes to cooks of all skill levels. Her passion is to demystify cooking so that anyone can whip up a simple and satisfying meal. Rachael is also a mom of two and uses her firsthand experience feeding young people to inspire our work on recipes like **Sweet and Sour Drumsticks** (p. 325) **and Sit On It Niçoise Sandwich** (p. 371). She's also been a clutch recipe-tester for this book.

Find out more about Rachael
@cookingwithrachael • www.cookingwithrachael.com

ALLIE RUDNEY

Allie is a health coach currently living in California. She's always had a passion for staying active and helping others get healthy, and that includes our four-legged friends. Allie dedicates her time to helping street dogs through her non-profit company Mila's Treats. As a vegetarian, friend and fellow dog-lover, she was a natural fit to collaborate on this book. I called on Allie to help with the Tasty Veggies Chapter. For recipes she inspired, see **1, 2, 3, 4, 5 Ingredient Meatless Meals** on p. 235.

Find out more about Allie
www.cravehealthcoach.com

TO YOU, THE PARENT ABOUT TO TAKE YOUR CHILDREN ON A JOURNEY IN THE KITCHEN...

Welcome to *Cooking with Mother Goose*, a cookbook I wrote for my kids and yours.

What lies ahead are memories, lots of little messes and a renewed relationship between your little ones, cooking and food.

In our home, food is the beginning of adventure. It's where we learn about other cultures, how to be brave and to try things we're unsure of at first. It's where it's OK to get our hands dirty. It's where we fill our tummies with yummy foods and our hearts with happy memories.

I hope this book brings some of that magic to you and your family too.

If you're motivated and ready to dive right in to cooking, go ahead and skip forward a couple of pages, directly to the "How to Use This Book" section. Reading that first will ensure you and your family get the most out of this book.

If you're still wondering who I am and why I spent the last two years elbow-deep in nursery rhymes and cooking (lots and lots of cooking), then please allow me to introduce myself and my silly, sometimes chaotic, but oh-so-beautiful little family.

FROM LEFT TO RIGHT: AXEL, LACEY, REX AND MY HUSBAND, TODD

A LITTLE BIT ABOUT MY FAMILY

I'm a parent just like you. I want the same things for my kids that you want for yours: happiness, health and the certainty that they are loved more than they could ever comprehend. And, of course, I want them to have the healthiest possible relationship with food.

My boys, Rex and Axel, are at the center of Todd's (my husband) and my world. Our four-legged children are just as much a part of our family too—Santo is our little Chihuahua and Barbie is our giant Doberman (together they make a funny pair). That's us! And at the center of how we connect and spend time together is food.

I grew up in New Orleans, Louisiana and until recently, we lived in Santiago, Chile. Now we live in Florida, but you'll find a lot of Creole and South American influence in my recipes.

By education and profession, I'm a Registered Dietitian Nutritionist and have been since 2014 when I found my passion for family and childhood nutrition. I've always believed that, as a dietitian, I have to know how to prepare food to teach people about nutrition and cooking. At the end of the day, my favorite way to support families is by balancing eating with enjoyment.

Cooking with Mother Goose is my third parent-child cookbook and nutrition handbook. The first two, *Eat! Play! Cook!* and *¡Vamos a Cocinar!* are directed to beginner eaters 6 months old and up. These books represent the culmination of my experience, education and love of spending time in the kitchen and at the table with my family.

REX, AXEL, ZOEY AND SOREN
READING MOTHER GOOSE STORIES

WHY MOTHER GOOSE?

The idea came to me one night during our bedtime routine. I'm guessing that like you, reading to my kids before bed has been important since they were born. One night, as we read through *Peas Porridge Hot, Little Jack Horner,* and *Peter, Peter Pumpkin Eater,* it struck me just how many Mother Goose rhymes involve food.

Maybe the connection came to me because I'm a dietitian, or maybe my mind drifted to the kitchen because I love to cook—and eat!—tasty foods. Whatever the reason, drift it did, and that's when the idea for this book was born.

So, I got to work, reading and thinking about those classic nursery rhymes and creating recipes that bring food from Mother Goose's world into ours.

Each one of the recipes is inspired by a rhyme. I let Mother Goose be my guide as I challenged not just my culinary- but my dietitian-mom mind to dream up new dishes. Some inspirations are quite literal: Cole Slaw for *Old King Cole* and Plum Cake to celebrate *Handy Pandy.*

With other rhymes, I became a bit more creative—the knife-wielding farmer's wife in *Three Blind Mice* inspired chopped salads, while *Aiken Drum* suggested Sweet and Sour Drumsticks.

The goal of this book is straightforward and the benefits are infinite: to bring parents and their littles together around food and cooking. From reducing risks of childhood obesity to ensuring a happy relationship with food into adulthood— coming together to experience meals from preparation to final plate carves out space for adventure, imagination, love and nourishment in all its forms.

Throughout this book, you'll find a variety of ways to involve your child in making meals. From reading the rhymes together and experiencing food with all five senses, to helping prep ingredients, I hope these recipes will nurture your family long after your children leave Mother Goose behind in favor of more rigorous literature.

I'll see you in the kitchen,

NUTRITION: CREATING HEALTHY RELATIONSHIPS WITH FOOD

Teaching children and parents how to eat well is what I do for a living—it's my profession and my passion. And I believe a baseline level of understanding about our relationship to food helps parents create an environment of health and enjoyment for their children. Kids learn more about food and eating during this time than at any other time in their life. For this reason, allow me to briefly explain the behaviors, attitudes, beliefs, norms and routines that we can model to our children in a way that encourages them to take the lead and eat intuitively.

BUILDING A FRAMEWORK OF TRUST

Feeding your kids is an 18-year job (if not longer). I've helped families around the world find success with a framework known as the **Division of Responsibility (DOR)**. Initially developed by Ellyn Satter, RDN, this system helps children learn to trust their hunger cues and fuel up according to how they feel.

With clear roles for parent and child, you'll find adopting the DOR as a family establishes healthy habits that last.

Here's how it goes...

PARENTS, IT'S OUR JOB to FEED. WE DECIDE:

What will we eat?

Our kids rely on us to feed them. Give children a variety of foods—offer different colors and categories at each meal, focusing on whole grains, animal or plant proteins, fruits and vegetables. When choosing what to feed your family, place a mix of familiar and unfamiliar foods on the table. Your child should always recognize two or three items. Keep in mind each meal should include at least three food groups. This way, your child will have access to eat food from all five food groups during the day.

When will we eat?

Find a routine that works for your family. Predictable meal schedules help kids learn what to expect and build feelings of security. Since children know when they will eat next, they are less anxious about food. Plus, children come to the table hungry when they don't eat between scheduled snacks and meals. Trust them to eat if they are hungry and until they are satisfied. A note on meal timing: young children (2-to 6-year-olds) typically need to eat every 2 to 3 hours; older kids (7 years and up) every 3 to 4 hours. A final piece of advice: don't try to feed a child when he or she is not hungry. Respect your meal times (the "when") and discourage grazing in between.

Where will we eat?

Structured meals and sit-down snacks are the cornerstones of the DOR from the time your little joins the family at the table until he or she leaves home. Today's fast-paced lifestyle and jam-packed days can make eating together a challenge, but it is so worth the effort. Sit-down meals, without distractions (avoid toys and anything with a screen), encourage mindfulness and connectedness. Eating together can happen at breakfast, lunch or dinner - or even at snacktime. Choose the meal(s) that gives you the most time to talk and connect. Eat as a family as often as you can to reap the many health and social benefits.

Bottom line, creating the environment our littles need to eat and stay in tune with their bodies is our job as parents. By following a framework of trust, I've found that my kiddos generally come to the table hungry, eat what I put out for them and are continuously building their healthy relationship with food. Of course, it takes time and patience to adapt to this system of feeding and we don't always get it right. But research shows that, in addition to the benefits mentioned above, eating together leads to more body confidence, fewer eating disorders and even higher literacy rates—reading Mother Goose with your children will help in that department too!

IT'S A CHILD'S JOB TO EAT. THEY DECIDE:

Whether (If) they eat or not.

A child gets to decide, "Am I going to eat this food?". And, as parents know all too well, children also decide if they aren't going to eat it. As hard as it may seem to put the choice in their hands, I encourage you to stick with it. Even the most stubborn children will not let themselves go hungry for long. Remember, there should always be a familiar food on the table that they can eat (see **What will we eat?**). By the way, kids often need up to 20 exposures to a food before they decide to try it and even more before deciding if they like it or not. Sometimes littles like new foods instantly; other times, they learn to love new foods through repeated exposure and modeled behavior. (**Tip:** *Parents, your kids are more likely to try food they see you eating.*) Some foods your kids may never like. And guess what? All of these outcomes are okay—preferences are personal. Just keep in mind that cooking together increases the likelihood of your child trying (and liking) new foods.

How much they're going to eat.

Your child is the one who determines, "Am I ravenous or just a little hungry?". So, try serving meals family-style instead of pre-plating food for your child. You can always help kids as they serve themselves. And parents, please don't stress about your child's daily intake (unless there is a known feeding issue such as over- or under-eating). Your child's stomach is only the size of his fist. It can't hold very much food at one time, which is why children eat smaller meals more often.

Some "rules of thumb" on food servings (check out the visual on the next page):

1. Toddler (children up to 3 years old) serving sizes should be about a quarter of an adult serving size. It can help if you don't put the whole portion on their plate at once because lots of food can be overwhelming. Instead, offer a few tablespoons at a time.
2. Let older children plate their food, so they have control over how much of each item goes on their plate. A typical serving is still about a quarter of an adult's. Unlike toddlers, "big kids" can handle seeing more food on their plate at once.

CLOSED FIST

A closed fist is about the recommended size for a serving of pasta, rice, cereal, vegetables and fruit.

PALM OF HAND

A meat or protein serving should be about as big as the palm of your open hand.

NUTRITION: CREATING HEALTHY RELATIONSHIPS WITH FOOD

Look at the photo on the left.

See the size difference between the little hand and the grown-up one?
Little hands need less food, bigger hands need more food.

SERVINGS OR PORTIONS

Most recipes in this book are shown plated in their entirety to encourage parents to serve meals family-style since it brings the family together and different members will need different portions.

The amount that you eat is called a *portion*. The yield of the recipe is measured in *servings*. You can have one serving, two servings or even four servings as your portion. That's up to you and how hungry you are.

If your children see you eating appropriate portions of all the food groups, they will do it too. So being a good role model benefits everyone!

Use the measurement tools you've got on your own body to help inform your portion sizes and show your littles how they can too!

NUTRITION: CREATING HEALTHY RELATIONSHIPS WITH FOOD

Establishing your roles as "feeders and eaters" takes practice. Be consistent and thoughtful. Over time, you'll find that mealtimes will lose their edge and eating together will be more relaxed.

Use this chart to help guide your feeding efforts.

INSTEAD OF...   TRY THIS...

INSTEAD OF...	TRY THIS...
Getting frustrated when your child says "I don't want this for lunch today." "I want _____."	Respond with, "That's not on the menu today. Would you like to pick a day to have _____?"
Telling your child to "try a little bit of everything" whether they want it or not.	Allow them to decide. Say, "That's OK, you don't have to eat it. Can you tell me what that food feels, smells and looks like instead?"
Placing food on your child's plate for them.	Serve meals family-style and allow children to fill their plate based on their own level of hunger.
Letting potential food waste make you want to reference the starving kids elsewhere in the world.	Ask your little, "Which two of these foods do you want to eat for lunch tomorrow?"

HOW TO USE THIS BOOK

Combining you and your little's favorite Mother Goose rhyme with spending time in the kitchen is the whole purpose of this book. So that's where you should start, reading the rhymes together. Look at the pictures and talk about what you see. What looks good to eat? Read the ingredients and the instructions aloud, too. Your child will learn new vocabulary words related to food and cooking. And hearing your voice will connect the nourishment of the recipe to the activity you'll do with your child.

STARTS WITH:

Reading the nursery rhyme with your little one.

FOLLOWED BY:

Delicious recipes that bring the rhyme to your table.

INCLUDES:

Essential information on how to go about feeding your family with tips on how to involve kids.

BONUS:

Encouraging imagination, exploration, personalization, discovery of language, foods and fine motor skills—***ALL*** things that are good for kids' development.

HOW TO USE THIS BOOK

MOUTH WATERING
FOOD PHOTOS

NUTRITIONAL
BENEFIT

NUTRITION
NIBBLE

Bookending each day with fruits and vegetables helps ensure your child gets the amount she needs each day. This recipe is fun to make when lots of kids are around—each person can choose the toppings for their boat and sail a spoon into their mouth. Serve this as a fancy weekend breakfast to start the day off right, or fill a huge papaya and display the ship as a beautiful and edible centerpiece for parties.

RECIPE TITLE

RECIPE YIELD, ALLERGY INFO
AND DIET RESTRICTIONS

CHALLENGE LEVEL
AND COOKING TIMES

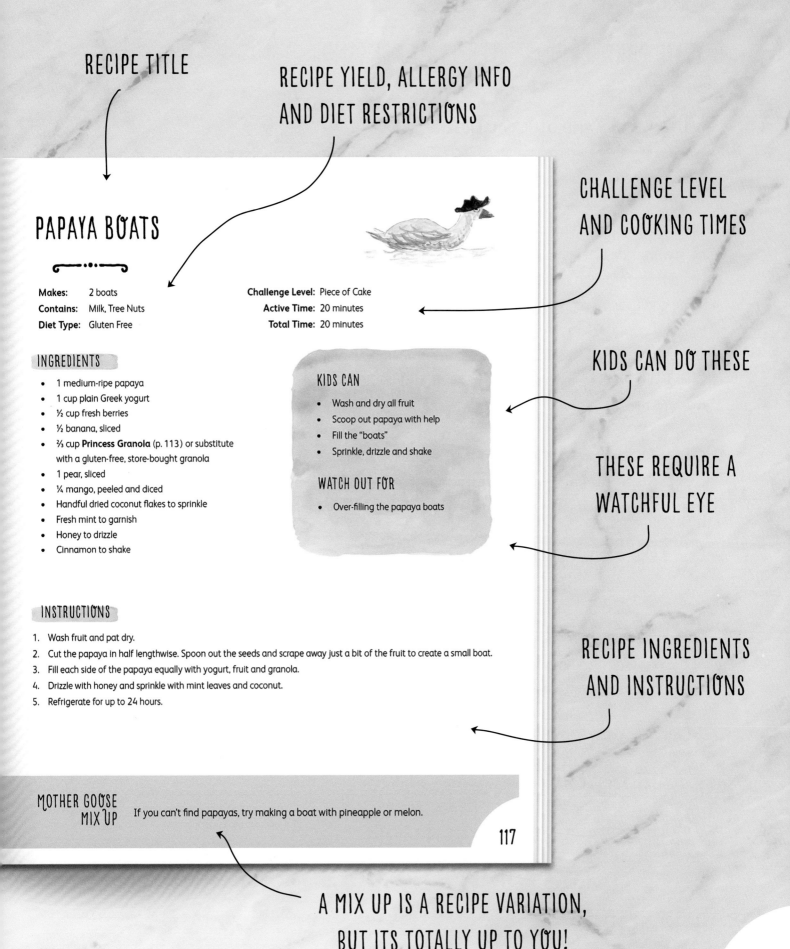

PAPAYA BOATS

Makes:	2 boats
Contains:	Milk, Tree Nuts
Diet Type:	Gluten Free

Challenge Level:	Piece of Cake
Active Time:	20 minutes
Total Time:	20 minutes

INGREDIENTS

- 1 medium-ripe papaya
- 1 cup plain Greek yogurt
- ½ cup fresh berries
- ½ banana, sliced
- ⅔ cup **Princess Granola** (p. 113) or substitute with a gluten-free, store-bought granola
- 1 pear, sliced
- ¼ mango, peeled and diced
- Handful dried coconut flakes to sprinkle
- Fresh mint to garnish
- Honey to drizzle
- Cinnamon to shake

KIDS CAN

- Wash and dry all fruit
- Scoop out papaya with help
- Fill the "boats"
- Sprinkle, drizzle and shake

WATCH OUT FOR

- Over-filling the papaya boats

KIDS CAN DO THESE

THESE REQUIRE A
WATCHFUL EYE

INSTRUCTIONS

1. Wash fruit and pat dry.
2. Cut the papaya in half lengthwise. Spoon out the seeds and scrape away just a bit of the fruit to create a small boat.
3. Fill each side of the papaya equally with yogurt, fruit and granola.
4. Drizzle with honey and sprinkle with mint leaves and coconut.
5. Refrigerate for up to 24 hours.

RECIPE INGREDIENTS
AND INSTRUCTIONS

MOTHER GOOSE
MIX UP   If you can't find papayas, try making a boat with pineapple or melon.

117

A MIX UP IS A RECIPE VARIATION,
BUT ITS TOTALLY UP TO YOU!

SOME PHRASES AND TERMS YOU'LL FIND

GLUTEN, DAIRY AND OTHER ALLERGENS

When applicable, I indicate if the recipe is gluten free, dairy free or contains any of the eight most common food allergens.

Gluten Free: Ingredients in the recipe are free from wheat, barley and rye. If a recipe includes oats, which can be cross-contaminated with gluten, I specify to buy certified gluten-free oats. For families following a gluten-free diet, please always check food labels thoroughly, as even some additives can contain gluten.

Dairy Free: Ingredients in the recipe are free from milk or animal-milk products such as butter, sour cream, yogurt or cheese. These recipes may include dairy-free alternatives such as almond milk, soy milk, or oil.

Contains Common Food Allergies: Ingredients in the recipe contain one or more of the eight common allergens. True food allergies are rare, but some foods are more likely to cause an allergic reaction than others. These eight foods cause around 90% of food allergies:

Milk	*Wheat*	*Tree Nuts*	*Shellfish*
Egg	*Fish*	*Peanuts*	*Soy*

For the convenience of the parent and safety of the child, I note when a recipe contains any of the eight most common allergens. Recipes that do not contain any of the eight common allergens will say: **Contains:** None of the Common Allergens.

If your child does not have a known allergy, there is no reason to avoid these foods.

SOME PHRASES AND TERMS YOU'LL FIND

CHALLENGE LEVEL

This indicates how much work is involved in making the recipe. There are three different categories.

Piece of Cake. This refers to easy recipes that are straightforward and forgiving. Sometimes they have quite a few steps but don't require a lot of attention.

Just a Pinch Involved. These are medium-easy recipes that require a bit more attention but often sound harder than they are. Once you make them a couple of times, they're a cinch.

So Worth the Effort. These recipes require some cooking experience but aren't hard *per se*. They are simply more involved. These are the types of recipes that will pay back in spades.

TIME

Active Time: The amount of time you'll be preparing and focused on cooking.

Total Time: The active time plus the passive time marinating, resting, baking, freezing, waiting for yeast to rise, etc.—this is the start to finish time.

NUTRITION NIBBLE

The "shout out" to why you should feel good about feeding this dish to your family. While all food has a place at your table, Nutrition Nibbles draw your attention to particularly valuable nutrition info or dietary advice. Creating balanced nutrition is about more than what we eat, so sometimes Nutrition Nibbles will explain strategies to support your child's journey of food discovery and acceptance.

MOTHER GOOSE MIX UP

Recipes are all about personalization. In the Mother Goose Mix Up, I share suggestions on ways to add a twist, but, please don't be limited by my ideas. Get creative. You and your little may discover something new and create a family classic!

KIDS CAN

WATCH OUT FOR

KIDS CAN

My favorite section! Here you'll find a short list of actionable tasks your child can do to get involved. These tasks are safe, engaging and fun. Kids can pop in and help and then go play. Or they can stay and 'supervise' your cooking from start to finish.

Remind children to wash their hands before and after preparing food, to wash vegetables and fruit before eating and not to mix ready-to-eat foods with foods that need to be cooked.

WATCH OUT FOR

Here is where I alert Mom and Dad about kitchen tools or processes that require a watchful eye. For example, hot surfaces and sharp knives. This section helps you, the adults, pay attention to potential hazards so you can avoid them. Getting burned or cut puts an end to the fun fast!

TIPS

Years of cooking, talking and teaching have taught me a thing or two about shortcuts that work and what other people I admire do to make life easier in the kitchen. I happily share these with you.

SETTING THE TABLE

Kids who aren't ready to cook can still help!

We always need someone to help set the table. For detailed instructions on proper table setting, see pages 48 and 49.

When you make something really tasty from this book, please share a photo or story with me. You can email me at mothergoose@storybooknutrition.com or tag @storybooknutrition on Instagram. With your permission, I'll share your accomplishments with others on my social media so everyone can enjoy and benefit from your "aha moment"!

SOME PHRASES AND TERMS YOU'LL FIND

COOKING "LACEY-ISMS" IN THIS BOOK

Blow-on-it-hot: The hottest temperature your mouth can stand. Some foods taste better fresh out of the pot or pan. Blow on each bite, test with your tongue and eat as soon as it is cool enough for you.

Handful: The amount of food (herbs, leafy greens, nuts or chocolate chips) that a child or parent can grab with one hand. It is generally expected to be ¼ to ½ cup.

Spoon Test: Coat the back of a spoon with a sauce and run your finger through it. If your finger leaves a path, the sauce, glaze or curd is ready.

Straight-from-the-fridge-cold: the temperature of an ingredient, like butter, when it comes out of the refrigerator, about 35°F to 38°F.

Toothpick Test: To see if your baked item is ready to come out of the oven, insert a toothpick into the center of the deepest section. If the toothpick comes out clean or with only a few crumbs, remove the dish from the oven and set it on a cooling rack. If the toothpick comes out with wet dough stuck to it, reset the timer and bake longer. Use the Toothpick Test when baking cakes, muffins, breads and cookies.

COOKING ASSUMPTIONS

In this book, you can always assume the following	
Eggs	Always large
Juice of a lemon	2 tablespoons of juice
Zest of a lemon	1 tablespoon of zest
1 garlic clove minced	1 teaspoon of fresh minced garlic (or ¼ teaspoon powdered garlic)
Shallots	1 small shallot = 2 tablespoons minced or sliced
Stick of butter	8 tablespoons or 115 grams (I use unsalted butter in all of my recipes)
Tablespoon	Approximately 15 milliliters
Teaspoon	Approximately 5 milliliters
Baking	Always convection bake setting

UTENSILS: WHAT YOU'LL NEED

I've moved my kitchen halfway around the world and back again. Out of necessity and opportunity, I've streamlined my equipment and don't have a lot of fancy gadgets or gizmos. But the ones I have kept, I consider to be my "other babies."

For some, this portfolio of kitchen accessories may be aspirational, while others will notice that my equipment isn't as nice as theirs. These tools are useful to have, but don't feel like you have to run out and buy new devices. Just use 'em if you got 'em. And please know that no matter what you've got in your kitchen, you can still prepare delicious foods without expensive gadgets. While it may be faster to chop using a food processor, you can always cut food by hand with a good knife. And while there are lots of options for adults based on your personal preference, I do suggest getting the kid-friendly tools (flagged in green) to keep cooking safe and fun for the littles.

Whether you're setting up a kitchen for the first time or simply want to do more cooking, having the basic gear for you and your child is an essential part of success.

Apple Corer

Blender

Box Grater

Bread Pan / Casserole Dish

Cake Frosting Scraper

Cake Pans (2 x 6 inch)

Cake Turntable

Cast Iron Skillet

Cheesecloth

Chef's Knife for Kids

Cocottes

Cooling Rack

Cutting Boards

Digital Infrared Thermometer

Food Processor

Frosting Spatula

Garlic Twister

Icing Bag and Tips

Kid-Safe Scissors

Kids Apron

Kitchen Mechanical Timer

Kitchen Scale

Lemon squeezer

Measuring Cups

Measuring Spoons

Mesh Strainer

Mixing Bowl

Mortar and Pestle

Muffin Tin

Nonstick Frying Pan

Pie Plate

Rolling Pin

Rubber Spatula / Scraper

Salad Spinner

Saucepan

Serving Spoons

Sheet pans in various sizes

Sifter

Silicone Baking Mat

Silicone Brush

Silicone Gummy Bear Mold

Silpat

Slow Cooker

Spiralizer

Springform Pans

Stand-Up Mixer

Stockpot

Strainer / Colander

Vegetable Brush

Vegetable Peeler

Wavy Chopper Cutter

Whisk

Wide, Deep Pot

Wire Mesh Spider

Wok

Zester / Microblade

Phone, notebook, pens and sticky pads to take pictures, make notes and call friends to come over and eat!

KNIFE CUTS

To make you look like a pro and expand your culinary vocabulary, I've included the most common knife cuts with a brief explanation of how to do them and a picture of how they look. I chopped everything with the kid-friendly chef's knife, and you can too. Come back and reference this page whenever you encounter a knife cut you are unsure about.

If you want to "sharpen" your knife skills, I listed a few of the recipes where you will find specific cuts.

I will admit that I am not a speed chopper. I like to think that my chef friends, Lorena and Rachael, find it endearing how slow or imprecise I can be (I am either fast and sloppy or slow and perfect) when I cut ingredients. Whenever possible, I "cheat" and pull out a food processor to finely chop herbs or use my garlic twister to mince garlic. But when that's not an option, here's all you need to know to do it the low-tech way.

SLICE

To cut something into even-sized, thin pieces using a sharp knife or food processor. You'll cut the item into coins (like a carrot), feathers (in the case of an onion), or crescent moons in the case of a seeded cucumber or celery stalk.

DICE

To cut small uniform cubes of any solid ingredient, for example, cheese or carrots. First, cut the food into even-sized thick strips and then slice crosswise into cubes.

MEDIUM DICE

To cut into cubes smaller than playing dice, but not brunoise. Cut carrots and celery to medium dice in **Chicken and Dumplings** (p. 329).

BRUNOISE

To cut small (⅛ inch) uniform cubes of any solid ingredient. This is a fine dice. You can cut the mango in the **Mango Pomegranate Salad** (p. 303) to brunoise.

GRATE

This cut doesn't involve a knife, but instead a box grater. Grate the cheese before making **Black and White Pasta Alfredo** (p. 215).

ZEST

To remove the colored outer layer of citrus from the rind. You'll need a zester or microblade to zest lemon peels and other citrus fruits. Small amounts of zest contain the essential oil of the fruit and give a strong characteristic flavor of the fruit to a dish. I also use a microblade to finely grate ginger.

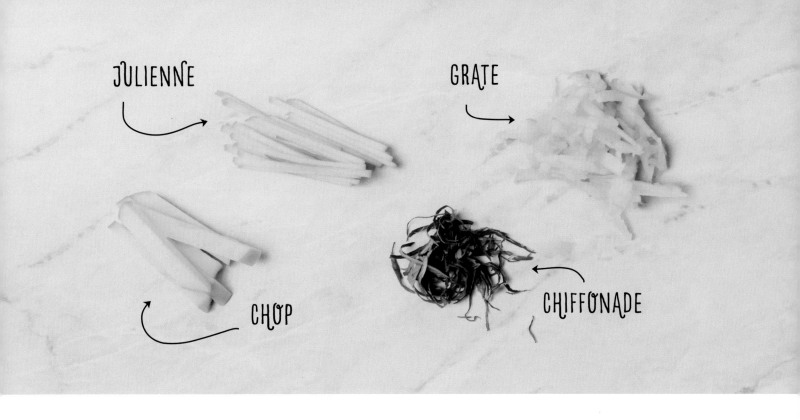

JULIENNE

GRATE

CHOP

CHIFFONADE

MINCE

To cut into very fine, even pieces using a sharp knife, a food processor or a mincer (used most often for garlic and herbs). This knife cut is found throughout the book. You can also use a garlic press or garlic twister to mince.

CHOP

Roughly cut food into small, even-sized pieces using a knife or food processor. When you make **Apple Butter** (p. 81), you "chop" the apples and then purée later.

WEDGES

Cut into segments, mostly used with tangerines or mandarin oranges (**King Cole's Slaw** p. 293) or pumpkin (**Honey-Spiced Roasted Pumpkin** p. 261).

BATON CUT

Square off the fruit or vegetable, then cut into rectangles. You will use this cut when you make **Three Ingredient Zucchini Fingers** (p. 241).

JULIENNE CUT

Square off fruit or vegetable then cut into the shape of matchsticks. You can master this cut when you make **Celery Slaw** (p. 289).

CHIFFONADE CUT

This ribbon cut is used for cutting leaves like chard or basil. You roll the leaf or stack of leaves into a tube and then make horizontal cuts, so when the leaf unrolls, you have a pretty ribbon. You'll roll and ribbon chard in **Team Chicken Soup** (p. 181).

CUPS OR GLASSES GO IN THE
TOP RIGHT-HAND CORNER
ABOVE THE KNIFE TIP.

LAY A PLATE IN FRONT OF
EACH CHAIR AT THE TABLE

PLACE THE FORK,
POINTY SIDE UP,
ON TOP OF THE NAPKIN.

SET THE SPOON,
SCOOP SIDE UP,
OUTSIDE OF THE KNIFE.

FOLD NAPKINS IN HALF,
THEN SET FOLDED NAPKIN
ON THE LEFT SIDE
OF THE PLATE.

THE PLATE IS
THE CENTER
OF EACH SETTING.

PLACE THE TABLE KNIFE
(CUTTING SIDE FACING IN)
ON THE RIGHT SIDE
OF THE PLATE.

SETTING THE TABLE

Setting the table is a great way to get buy-in on meals — it reminds kids that mealtime is coming. Use this activity to help them transition from playing so they can wash their hands and get ready to eat something yummy!

For the most part, kids can set the table by themselves if they can access all the "ingredients" and reach the table.

In our house, we keep the kids' plates and all the (safe) silverware in low drawers. This way, Axel and Rex can reach what they need, choose the dishware and set the table while I finish up cooking. Since their dinnerware is kid-friendly, if they drop plates, cups or flatware—it isn't a big deal. We just pick them up, wipe them off and try again.

TIME TO GET STARTED

Now, you've got all you need to get started *Cooking with Mother Goose*!

Just a quick word about the recipes you're about to prepare. The title and page number of every nursery rhyme are highlighted in ***bold italic*** so you can read the inspiration for each recipe before you make it.

I've organized the recipes into sections that make sense for the way my family eats but don't be intimidated by a label. Many recipes fit into more than one category, and hey, if you want **Ratatouille Lasagna** for breakfast and a **Cinnamon Roll** for dessert, go for it.

The only rules when it comes to what you eat and when are the rules you make...

No judgments. Enjoy!

CHAPTER THREE
SLURPY SOUPS

CHAPTER 1

Reference Recipes

When I started my culinary journey, I learned to always have some basics on hand. Sandwiches made with a smear of apple and nut butter or pasta with pesto are easy enough for the babysitter to put together and can be ready fast.

These recipes, which include butters, grains and pastas and some yummy, nourishing broths always save my bacon and provide inspiration for last-minute meals.

OLD MOTHER HUBBARD

OLD MOTHER HUBBARD

Old Mother Hubbard
Went to the cupboard
To give her poor dog a bone;
But when she came there,
Her cupboard was bare,
And so the poor dog had none.

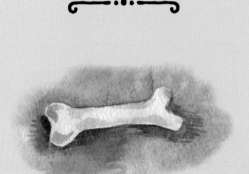

VEGETABLE BROTH AND OTHER STOCKS

Homemade bone stocks and vegetable broth are chock full of flavor
without the additives you find in store-bought broth and bouillon cubes.
Making them is surprisingly easy and allows you to recycle and reuse
what you might otherwise throw away. The only thing stocks and broths
require are time, a big, deep pot or slow cooker, leftover bones and some
basic vegetables (wilted or in perfect shape). Plus, they freeze well,
so make one recipe, portion it out and save the rest!

NUTRITION NIBBLE Bone stocks become gel-like when cool. Jiggling is a good thing! Gelatin in the broth allows our bodies to use more of the complete protein we eat. The gelatin also makes food cooked using broth easier to digest, helping heal the gut by soothing and lining the mucous membrane. This is why we crave "brothy" soups when we are sick or after a major athletic accomplishment—like running a marathon. The nutrient-dense liquid helps us heal... and it tastes so good!

CHICKEN STOCK

Makes: 12 cups

Contains: None of the Common Allergens

Diet Type: Gluten Free, Dairy Free

Challenge Level: Piece of Cake

Active Time: 30 minutes

Total Time: 12 hours (maximum)

Stock is made by simmering bones and vegetables for 8 to 12 hours and is packed with concentrated nutrition and flavor.

INGREDIENTS

- Leftover bones from 1 to 3 roasted chickens (the more bones the better)
- 2 carrots
- 2 stalks celery including leaves
- 2 yellow onions
- 1 head garlic
- 1 bay leaf
- Black peppercorns
- 2 tablespoons apple cider vinegar
- A few fresh sprigs or a pinch of dried thyme
- Filtered water to cover all the bones

KIDS CAN

- Wash produce
- Count up to 12 hours when you set the slow cooker

WATCH OUT FOR

- Wash hands after handling old bones

INSTRUCTIONS

1. Put all the ingredients in your slow cooker in the order above.
2. Set slow cooker to low heat and cook for 8 to 12 hours, the longer you cook the more concentrated the flavors will be. (*Tip: This is a great recipe to set up before bed.*)
3. Pass contents of the slow cooker through a strainer or mesh sieve before portioning into separate containers.
4. Store in refrigerator for up to 4 days, or freeze and use for up to 2 months.

MOTHER GOOSE MIX UP

There is no rule saying chicken bones are the only ones that make good broth. Swap in a mix of lamb bones, rib bones, and/or T-bones for a delicious twist!

VEGETABLE BROTH

Makes: 12 cups

Contains: None of the Common Allergens

Diet Type: Dairy Free

Challenge Level: Piece of Cake

Active Time: 30 minutes

Total Time: 12 hours (maximum)

INGREDIENTS

- 1 large onion, chopped
- 2 cloves garlic, smashed
- 3 medium carrots, chopped
- 2 stalks celery including tops, chopped
- 1 medium bell pepper or ½ red and ½ yellow, white parts and seeds removed
- 4 mushrooms, chopped
- Drizzle of extra virgin olive oil
- 1 bay leaf
- A few sprigs of parsley, thyme, rosemary, basil and oregano
- 1 tablespoon tomato paste, optional
- 7 to 8 cups filtered water

KIDS CAN

- Wash produce
- Count up to 12 hours when you set the slow cooker

WATCH OUT FOR

- Hearing the kids say they love veggies

INSTRUCTIONS

1. Coat slow cooker pot with olive oil.
2. Roughly chop the vegetables.
3. Add all ingredients to the slow cooker and fill with water until everything is covered.
4. Set slow cooker to low heat and cook for 8 to 12 hours.
5. Pass contents of slow cooker through a strainer before separating into smaller portions.
6. Use immediately. Store in refrigerator for up to 4 days, or freeze for up to 2 months.

NUTRITION NIBBLE Bone broths (also known as stocks) are a rich source of minerals and trace elements which are pulled from the vegetables, bone, marrow, cartilage and tendons as they cook.

FISH STOCK

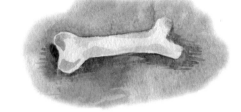

Makes: 12 cups	**Challenge Level:** Piece of Cake
Contains: Fish	**Active Time:** 1 hour
Diet Type: Gluten Free, Dairy Free	**Total Time:** 1 hour

Though used less often than meat broth, fish broth is equally as important for well-rounded palettes.

INGREDIENTS

- 1 white onion
- 1 carrot
- 3 cloves garlic
- 2 bay leaves
- 1 cup dry white wine (whatever you have on hand)
- 8 to 10 cups filtered water, divided
- 5 allspice berries (or generous shakes of ground allspice)
- 1 teaspoons anise seed (or 1 star anise)
- Fish head, gills removed

KIDS CAN

- Wash produce
- Count the cups of water

WATCH OUT FOR

- Wash hands after handling fish heads

INSTRUCTIONS

1. Place a large pot on the stove.
2. Roughly chop vegetables and add them to the pot with wine and 2 cups water.
3. Boil together for 20 minutes.
4. Add the fish head and an additional 6 to 8 cups cool water. Bring everything back to a boil.
5. Lower the heat and let stock simmer for 20 more minutes.
6. If a foam forms on the top, just scrape it off (or ignore it until the end).
7. Pour broth through a strainer. This removes all the vegetable and fish debris.
8. Store in the fridge for up to 4 days, or freeze and use for up to 2 months.

BLOW WIND, BLOW

BLOW WIND, BLOW

Blow wind, blow! And go mill, go!

That the miller may grind his corn;

That the baker may take it,

And into rolls make it,

And send us some hot in the morn.

NUTRITION
NIBBLE
What the heck is gluten anyway? Even with the gluten-free movement gaining popularity, many people are unsure. Gluten is the general name for the proteins found in wheat, barley and rye. Many store-bought, gluten-free flours are a blend of flours that don't have much nutritional value. **Blow Wind Blow Gluten-Free Flour Blend** boosts the nutritional content of the food you're making with it. It adds things like protein, vitamins, minerals and fiber to any recipe. Make the switch to making your own and use it as a 1:1 replacement for all-purpose flour.

BLOW WIND BLOW GLUTEN-FREE FLOUR BLEND

Makes:	3½ cups	**Challenge Level:**	Piece of Cake
Contains:	Tree Nuts (Almond Flour)	**Active Time:**	10 minutes
Diet Type:	Gluten Free	**Total Time:**	10 minutes

Living a gluten-free or gluten-light life is a reality for many families. While everyone in my family is fortunate enough to be gluten tolerant and free from celiac disease (an auto-immune disease treated only by avoiding gluten), we are aware of the challenges many of our friends face. Having a gluten-free flour blend at your fingertips comes in handy. I don't recommend using this flour for breads, but this blend will work perfectly with **Chinese Egg Cake Muffins** (p. 103), **Cake Donuts with Mulberry Glaze** (p. 159) and **Yogurt Plumcake with Plum Glaze** (p. 163). I promise your gluten-free effort will be appreciated.

INGREDIENTS

*(**Tip**: Make sure all the alternative flour ingredients have the Gluten-Free Certification.)*

- 1½ cups brown rice flour
- ¼ cup tapioca flour
- ½ cup coconut flour
- ¼ cup oat flour
- ½ cup almond flour
- 1 to 1½ teaspoons xanthan gum
  *(**Tip**: This helps keep our baked goods from falling apart on us!)*

KIDS CAN

- Touch the different flours and compare their textures
- Sift the different flours to remove lumps
- Wipe down the counter with a damp cloth after you're done

WATCH OUT FOR

- Sneezes, big sighs, giggles spilling some flour is inevitable but not dangerous

INSTRUCTIONS

1. Measure each flour. (***Tip:** the best way to measure flour is to spoon it into a measuring cup and then level-off the measuring cup with the spoon handle.*)
2. Sift flours together into a large bowl.
3. Use immediately or store in an airtight container in the pantry.

HOCUS POCUS

HOCUS POCUS

Hocus Pocus!
Alakazam!
Abracadabra!
I think you can
Use *Please* and *Thank You,*
These words too,
Just like magic
Make wishes come true!

PRESTO PESTO

—— · • · ——

Makes:	About 2 cups	**Challenge Level:**	Piece of Cake
Contains:	Milk, Tree Nuts	**Active Time:**	15 minutes
Diet Type:	Gluten Free	**Total Time:**	15 minutes

Presto Pesto makes my reference recipes list because there are so many ways to use it: served on pasta, stirred into mashed potatoes, smeared on sandwiches or as a dip.

INGREDIENTS

- Bunch of basil, about 2 cups, packed
- 2 garlic cloves
- ½ cup extra virgin olive oil
- 2 handfuls toasted walnuts or pine nuts
  (*Tip: Pine nuts are not available everywhere. Walnuts are an easy-to-find and more economical option.*)
- ½ cup Parmesan cheese, grated
- 1 teaspoon lemon juice or white vinegar
- Pinch of salt

KIDS CAN

- Wash and spin basil in salad spinner
- Separate basil leaves from stems
- Twist the garlic twister to mince garlic
- Squeeze lemon

WATCH OUT FOR

- Sharp blades of the food processor can be dangerous for little hands

INSTRUCTIONS

1. Rinse and spin basil. Separate the leaves from the stems. Discard stems.
2. Combine all ingredients in a food processor. Pulse until smooth.

MOTHER GOOSE MIX UP

Add a ripe avocado to make pesto even creamier. Perfect for dips and spreads.

LITTLE TOMMY TUCKER

LITTLE TOMMY TUCKER

Little Tommy Tucker
Sings for his supper,
What shall we give him?
White bread and butter.
How shall he cut it
Without e're a knife?
How shall he marry
Without e're a wife?

PEANUT

ALMOND

PUMPKIN SEED
"PEPITA"

NUT BUTTER

Makes: About 1 cup

Contains: Peanuts, Tree Nuts (optional)

Diet Type: Gluten Free, Dairy Free

Challenge Level: Piece of Cake

Active Time: 10 minutes

Total Time: 10 minutes

In addition to various nuts, try making butters from sunflower seeds and pumpkin seeds—a handy option when you have a child or classroom with nut allergies. When making butter from seeds or nuts you may need to add oil to help your food processor obtain a smooth and spreadable consistency. For the best flavor, add the oil that comes from the nut or seed. (For example, when I make pumpkin seed butter, I add pumpkin oil. To peanut butter, I add peanut oil and so on). Spread these butters on bread to make sandwiches, smear onto apples or celery or use in **Spaghetti Squash Shrimp Pad Thai** (p. 347).

INGREDIENTS

- 2 cups peanuts
- Peanut oil as needed (up to 2 tablespoons)

KIDS CAN

- Scoop peanuts
- Push button on food processor with supervision

WATCH OUT FOR

- Sharp blades of the food processor

INSTRUCTIONS

1. Place several handfuls of roasted, shelled peanuts or nut of your choice in a food processor. Pulse in several increments until smooth. Allow the food processor motor to rest in between.

2. Some nuts have less natural oil so you may need to add extra oil to help your food processor along. Slowly drizzle in oil while the food processor is running to help turn the nuts into a spreadable paste.

3. Transfer to a jar with a tight-fitting lid.

4. Store in refrigerator for up to 1 month.

USE THIS APPLE BUTTER RECIPE FOR CINNAMON ROLLS ON PAGE 171.

APPLE BUTTER

Makes: 4 to 5 cups

Contains: None of the Common Allergens

Diet Type: Gluten Free, Dairy Free

Challenge Level: Just a Pinch Involved

Active Time: 30 minutes

Total Time: 2 hours

INGREDIENTS

- 8 medium apples, peeled and coarsely chopped
- 1½ cups apple cider or apple juice
- ½ cup packed brown sugar
- ⅓ cup dark molasses
- 2¼ teaspoons ground cinnamon
- ¾ teaspoon ground nutmeg
- ½ teaspoon ground cloves
- ¼ teaspoon ground ginger
- 1 tablespoon lemon juice

KIDS CAN

- Wash apples and pat dry
- Smell spices
- Squeeze lemon

WATCH OUT FOR

- Hot pans and stove
- Sharp blades in the blender

INSTRUCTIONS

1. In a large saucepan, combine apples, apple cider, brown sugar, molasses, cinnamon, nutmeg, cloves and ginger.
2. Bring to a boil.
3. Reduce heat and simmer, uncovered. Stir often.
4. When mixture reaches a thick, spreadable consistency, remove from heat. This takes about 1½ hours.
5. Squeeze on lemon juice and stir. When cool enough to touch, mash apples with the back of a spoon.
6. Transfer to a blender and pulse in batches until apple butter is smooth.
7. Store apple butter in several airtight containers in the refrigerator.

    You can also freeze jars of apple butter for up to 6 months for later use.

CHARLEY PARLEY

CHARLEY PARLEY

Charley Parley stole the barley
Out of the baker's shop.
The baker came out,
and gave him a clout,
Which made poor Charley hop.

BASIC HULLED BARLEY:
RICH IN MANY
BENEFICIAL NUTRIENTS

WHOLE GRAIN (BROWN) RICE:
WHOLE GRAINS ARE MORE
NUTRITIOUS AND STILL GLUTEN FREE

CLASSIC COUSCOUS:
READY IN MINUTES

BASIC BULGUR: A VERSATILE, JACK-OF-ALL TRADES
GRAIN ADAPTABLE TO BREAKFAST, LUNCH OR DINNER

QUINOA: CONTAINS
ALL 9 ESSENTIAL
AMINO ACIDS

WHITE RICE: EASY TO DIGEST,
NATURALLY GLUTEN FREE

LONG GRAIN WHITE RICE

Makes: 4 cups

Contains: None of the Common Allergens

Diet Type: Gluten Free, Dairy Free

Challenge Level: Piece of Cake

Active Time: 5 minutes

Total Time: 30 minutes

White rice is a simple carb, it's easy to digest—a gentle choice for sick tummies. In the USA and many other countries, white rice is enriched (that's a good thing!) with added nutrients, including iron and B vitamins like folic acid, niacin, thiamine and more.

INGREDIENTS

- 2 cups rice
- 3 cups filtered water

KIDS CAN

- Measure the rice and water

WATCH OUT FOR

- Hot stove top and escaping steam can burn

INSTRUCTIONS

1. Put rice and water together in a saucepan. Bring to a boil, then set a timer for 6 minutes.
2. When timer sounds, cover pot and reduce heat to low until rice is tender. Set a timer for 10 minutes more.
3. When the second timer sounds, remove the pot from the heat and let it stand for 10 minutes.
4. Fluff with a fork.
5. Serve immediately or store in an airtight container in the refrigerator for future use.

BASIC QUINOA

Makes: 3 cups

Contains: None of the Common Allergens

Diet Type: Gluten Free, Dairy Free

Challenge Level: Piece of Cake

Active Time: 5 minutes

Total Time: 30 minutes

INGREDIENTS

- 1 cup quinoa, rinsed
- 2 cups filtered water or stock
- Pinch of salt

KIDS CAN

- Rinse quinoa
- Fluff with a fork

WATCH OUT FOR

- Hot stove top
- Bubbling pot

INSTRUCTIONS

1. Put quinoa, water and salt together in a saucepan.
2. Bring to a simmer, then cover and cook over low heat until tender, about 15 minutes. Stir occasionally.
3. Remove from heat. Let stand covered for 10 minutes.
4. Fluff with a fork.
5. Use immediately or store in an airtight container in the refrigerator for future use.

NUTRITION NIBBLE

Quinoa is basically a seed, which is prepared and eaten similarly to a grain. It is gluten free, high in protein and one of the few plant foods that contain sufficient amounts of all nine essential amino acids. It is also high in fiber, magnesium, B vitamins, iron, potassium, calcium, phosphorus, vitamin E and beneficial antioxidants.

WHOLE GRAIN (BROWN) RICE

Makes: 3 cups

Contains: None of the Common Allergens

Diet Type: Gluten Free, Dairy Free

Challenge Level: Piece of Cake

Active Time: 15 minutes

Total Time: 1 hour 10 minutes

Brown rice takes some time to cook. Make extra and freeze it so you always have grains on hand. Just pop frozen brown rice in the microwave to defrost and move on with your recipe (like **Southwest Rice Salad** on page 231).

INGREDIENTS

- 1 cup brown rice
- 1 teaspoon extra virgin olive oil
  (or enough to cover the bottom of your pot)
- 1 teaspoon salt
- 2¼ cups filtered water or stock

KIDS CAN

- Rinse brown rice
- Fluff with fork

WATCH OUT FOR

- Bubbling pot and a hot stove

INSTRUCTIONS

1. Place an empty saucepan on medium heat. Warm it for about 2 minutes.
2. Meanwhile, pour dry rice in a colander and rinse well.
3. Add oil to warm pot and pour in rice. Toast rice until it starts to smell nutty.
4. Slowly add the water and salt. The water should steam off the toasted rice. Bring to a boil, then cover your pot and reduce heat to low.
5. Cook rice until all the liquid is gone, about 45 minutes. I usually start checking on it after 38 minutes.
6. Taste. If rice is crunchy, add a bit more water and cook another 10 minutes. If rice is chewy, remove rice from heat and allow to rest in it's covered pot for 10 to 15 minutes.
7. Fluff with a fork and serve.

NUTRITION NIBBLE Brown rice is the entire rice grain. It contains the fiber-rich bran, the nutrient-packed germ and the carbohydrate-rich endosperm.

CLASSIC COUSCOUS

Makes: 4 cups

Contains: Wheat

Diet Type: Dairy Free

Challenge Level: Piece of Cake

Active Time: 5 minutes

Total Time: 30 minutes

Did you know couscous isn't a grain? Those little granules are actually a type of pasta, made from semolina flour. Couscous is a traditional staple of North and West Africa and the Middle East, but it is eaten in many other parts of the world as well. It's a great companion to meat, stews and veggies of all kinds.

INGREDIENTS

- 1½ cups filtered water or stock
- 1 cup couscous

KIDS CAN

- Measure the couscous and water

WATCH OUT FOR

- Hot stove top and escaping steam can burn

INSTRUCTIONS

1. Use a ratio of 1½ cups of water per 1 cup of couscous. Multiply as needed for larger volume.
2. Bring the water to a boil either on the stove or in the microwave.
3. Pour the couscous into the boiling water, cover and let sit for 5 to 10 minutes.
4. When the granules have absorbed all the liquid, fluff the cooked couscous with a fork and serve.

BASIC BULGUR

Makes: 3 cups	**Challenge Level:** Piece of Cake	
Contains: Wheat	**Active Time:** 5 minutes	
Diet Type: Dairy Free	**Total Time:** 30 minutes	

Bulgur is a whole grain made from dried, cracked wheat. It is an especially good source of manganese, magnesium, iron, and fiber. You can make a batch of whole grain bulgur to enjoy in various forms for breakfast, lunch and dinner. If gluten free isn't important to you, swap cooked bulgur for oats in **Plum Porridge** (p. 125) for a delicious whole grain breakfast or use it to make **Avocado Tabbouleh** (p. 227) for lunch. Don't be afraid to throw a cup of cooked bulgur into soups to amp up the nutritional value.

INGREDIENTS

- 2 cups filtered water
- 1 cup uncooked bulgur
- 2 teaspoons extra virgin olive oil
- ½ teaspoon salt

KIDS CAN

- Measure bulgur
- Count cups of water
- Sprinkle salt

WATCH OUT FOR

- Hot stove

INSTRUCTIONS

1. Bring water to a boil in a medium saucepan over medium-high heat.
2. Stir in bulgur.
3. Cover and reduce heat to medium-low and simmer for 12 minutes.
4. Remove saucepan from heat and let stand covered for 10 minutes.
5. Uncover, drizzle with oil and sprinkle with salt.
6. Fluff with a fork to combine.
7. Refrigerate for up to 48 hours or freeze on the day of cooking once cooled.

BASIC HULLED BARLEY

Makes: 3½ cups

Contains: Wheat

Diet Type: Dairy Free

Challenge Level: Piece of Cake

Active Time: 5 minutes

Total Time: 45 minutes

INGREDIENTS

- 1 cup barley
- 3 cups filtered water

KIDS CAN

- Count cups of water
- Measure cups of barley

WATCH OUT FOR

- Hot stove
- Foaming pot

INSTRUCTIONS

1. Combine the barley and water in a large pot.
2. Bring to a boil over high heat. Keep an eye on the pot as barley gives off a lot of foam and can cause the pot to boil over.
3. When the barley reaches boiling, lower the heat to a low simmer, cover and continue to cook. Barley is done when it has tripled in volume and is soft, yet chewy. I start checking for doneness at 40 minutes.
   (**Tip**: Add more water if the pot becomes dry before the barley has finished cooking.)
4. When the barley is done, it will have absorbed most of the water. If there is a little water still left in the pot, let sit covered for 10 minutes, until all the water has absorbed. If there is a lot of water left, drain it out in a colander over the sink.
5. Fluff with a fork to separate the grains before serving.

NUTRITION NIBBLE

Almost all forms of barley utilize the whole grain. Barley is a particularly rich source of fiber and trace minerals such as molybdenum, manganese and selenium. It also contains decent amounts of copper, vitamin B1, chromium, phosphorus, magnesium and niacin.

CROOKED MAN

CROOKED MAN

There was a crooked man,
and he walked a crooked mile,
He found a crooked sixpence
against a crooked stile;
He bought a crooked cat
which caught a crooked mouse,
And they all lived together
in a little crooked house.

In our family, when people are hungry, things go sideways pretty
quickly. Behavior can change from the straight and narrow to,
well, crooked, when tummies start rumbling. When you're not sure
what to make for your "starving", grumpy family choose pasta.
It's quick, easy and there's almost always a box in the pantry.

"AL DENTE" MEANS "TO THE TOOTH".
THIS RECIPE'S NOODLES ARE COOKED
BUT LEFT WITH A BIT OF FIRMNESS.

PASTA (AL DENTE)

Makes: 4 cups

Contains: Wheat

Diet Type: Dairy Free

Challenge Level: Piece of Cake

Active Time: 5 minutes

Total Time: 15 minutes

How much pasta is enough? If that's all you're serving, my rule of thumb is 2 ounces (½ cup) of dry pasta makes enough cooked pasta (about 1 cup) to feed an adult.

INGREDIENTS

- 2 quarts filtered water
- Pinch of salt
- ½ pound dry pasta

KIDS CAN

- Use kid-safe scissors to open pasta bag with help
- Taste test rinsed noodles for firmness

WATCH OUT FOR

- Bubbling pot and a hot stove

INSTRUCTIONS

1. Put water and salt together in a large pot. Bring to a boil.
2. Add dry pasta, continue to boil uncovered, stirring often for 8 to 10 minutes.
3. Taste test the pasta a few minutes before the end of the suggested cooking time. Remember to rinse it off with cold water first.
4. If the pasta is chalky and crunchy, it is too raw and needs to continue boiling. If it is "al dente," it is ready.
5. Ladle out 1 cup of the starchy pasta water to use in sauces. Set aside.
6. Drain the cooking water and immediately toss the pasta together with your favorite sauce and some of the reserved cooking water.

MOTHER GOOSE MIX UP If you are using fresh pasta instead of dry, simply add the noodles to the boiling, salted water. Noodles will float when they are done, about 2 to 3 minutes. At this point, remove the pot from heat and drain the cooking water.

ZOODLES (OR ZUCCHINI NOODLES) ARE A FUN,
LOW-CARB SWAP FOR TRADITIONAL PASTA

ZOODLES

Makes: 2 cups

Contains: None of the Common Allergens

Diet Type: Gluten Free, Dairy Free

Challenge Level: Piece of Cake

Active Time: 10 minutes

Total Time: 15 minutes

INGREDIENTS

- 2 large zucchini or summer squash
- 1 teaspoon extra virgin olive oil

KIDS CAN

- Wash zucchini and pat dry

WATCH OUT FOR

- Sharp blades of a spiralizer
- Hot stove

INSTRUCTIONS

1. Wash zucchini and pat dry.

   (**Tip:** *I like zucchini and summer squash noodles, but beets and carrots can also be spiralized with care*).

2. Fit your zucchini to the hand spiralizer. Rotate to create Zoodles.

3. In a nonstick frying pan, heat olive oil over medium heat.

   Sauté veggie noodles for 3 or 4 minutes so they are firm but not raw.

4. Serve in place of, or mixed with, traditional pasta noodles for a boost of color and nutrition.

NUTRITION NIBBLE Making noodles from vegetables is an easy way to add more vegetables to your family's diet.

CHAPTER 2

Good Morning

Morning, Sunshine! As a mom, I know that giving my littles "five more minutes" of sleep is tempting, but as a dietitian, I know it's essential to give kids time to power up before they start their day.

Studies show that children who eat breakfast—even if it's just a few bites—do better in school, are more likely to participate in physical activities and eat healthier overall. Mornings can be hard, but these recipes give you 18 delicious reasons not to hit the snooze button. If your little one doesn't have a big appetite in the morning, try **Two-Bite Blueberry Muffins** (p. 107) or **Weekday Scrambled Eggs** (p. 137). As kids get used to waking up for breakfast, you'll find their morning appetite improves.

It really helps when our children participate in the kitchen, but I realize that there isn't extra time for mini-chefs on most weekday mornings—so if your little wants to get involved, make **Carrot Cake Overnight Oats** (p. 129) together the night before.

THE MUFFIN MAN

THE MUFFIN MAN

Oh, do you know the muffin man,
The muffin man, the muffin man,
Do you know the muffin man,
Who lives on Drury Lane?

Yes, I know the muffin man,
The muffin man, the muffin man,
Yes, I know the muffin man,
Who lives on Drury Lane.

We enjoy "The Muffin Man" as a game
while we wait for our muffins to bake. Here's how to play:

**Sit in a circle. The youngest child starts the game
by asking the child on his left.**

"Do you know the muffin man? The muffin man, the muffin man.
Do you know the muffin man who lives on Drury Lane"

The child on the left will respond by singing the next verse:
"Yes, I know the muffin man. The muffin man, the muffin man.
Oh, yes, I know the muffin man, who lives on Drury Lane."

Then both children sing together:
"Then two of us know the muffin man, the muffin man.
Yes, two of us know the muffin man, who lives on Drury Lane"

**Then the second child in the circle will address
the third child by singing:**
"Do you know the muffin man? The muffin man, the muffin man.
Do you know the muffin man who lives on Drury Lane"

**And the reply is sung together by the first,
second and third player:**
"Then three of us know the muffin man, the muffin man"....

The game continues until everyone in the circle is singing:
"We all know the Muffin Man..."

CHINESE EGG CAKE MUFFINS

Makes: 6 muffins or 12 mini muffins

Contains: Egg

Diet Type: Gluten Free, Dairy Free

Challenge Level: Piece of Cake

Active Time: 15 minutes

Total Time: 30 minutes

My boys like to eat these light, fluffy muffins for breakfast or as an after-school snack. The texture of these muffins resembles angel food cake—they are pale and light. These muffins will not turn golden in the oven, rather they stay white in color, so darkening is not an indication of doneness.

INGREDIENTS

- 2 eggs, room temperature
- 5 tablespoons **Blow Wind Blow Gluten-Free Flour Blend** (p. 71)
- 3 tablespoons granulated sugar
- ¾ to 1 teaspoon extra virgin olive oil
- Your favorite blend of spices
  (We like McCormick Chinese Five Spice blend)

KIDS CAN

- Crack eggs with help
- Sift flour
- Spray and line muffin pan

WATCH OUT FOR

- Hot oven

INSTRUCTIONS

1. In a large bowl, beat eggs and sugar together until creamy and pale yellow, about 5 to 7 minutes. Beat until there are no more bubbles.
2. Sift flour over the whisked egg bowl and fold in using a rubber spatula.
3. Add oil, fold in again.
4. Spray muffin tin with cooking spray and line with 6 homemade **Artisanal Muffin Liners** (p. 105).
5. Add 1 to 2 heaping tablespoons of fluffy batter into each liner.
6. Sprinkle generously with spice blend.
7. Bake at 350°F for 15 minutes or until they pass the "Toothpick Test."

NUTRITION NIBBLE

Projects like this one help children develop life skills through play and repetition. Using scissors is a mental and physical activity that helps develop strength and coordination. Cutting with scissors alone offers many benefits, including:

- Independent movements of fingers
- Strengthens hand muscles
- Two-handed coordination

- Eye-hand coordination
- Fine motor skills (separation of hand, finger dexterity)

- Promotes grasp pattern
- Focus and attention
- Visual perceptual tasks (directionality)

ARTISANAL MUFFIN LINERS

Makes: 8 to 12 liners

Challenge Level: Just a Pinch Involved

Active Time: 30 minutes

Total Time: 30 minutes

Make your homemade muffins look extra fancy by creating these easy liners from parchment paper.

INGREDIENTS

- Parchment paper
- Pencil
- Kid-safe scissors
- Ruler
- 1 rubber band
- Glass or jar small enough to fit inside your muffin tin
  (**Tip:** *the mouth of a champagne flute fits perfectly inside my muffin tin. Cheers!*)

KIDS CAN

- Do just about every step of this with the help of an adult

WATCH OUT FOR

- Sharp scissors
- Fragile glass
- Rubber bands that kids might like to fling

INSTRUCTIONS

1. Use the pencil and ruler to measure and draw a 5-inch square of parchment paper. Cut it out with kid-safe scissors.

2. Look at your first square. You will use this "pattern square" to make more squares.

3. Pull out a long strip of parchment paper.

4. Set the pattern square on top of the paper and trace it with a pencil. Carefully cut along the lines you drew. Aim to make 8 to 12 squares.

5. Ask an adult to help you place the center of the square on top of your glass and press firmly around all sides so that the paper bends around the top of the glass. Hold the paper in place with a rubber band. Set glass aside to give the paper a few minutes to set and create the muffin cup. (**Tip:** *This is a good time to make your batter.*)

6. When you are ready to use, remove the rubber band, place the liner in your muffin tin, fill halfway with batter and bake.

7. Don't worry if you spill or splatter batter on your liner. Cooked muffin splatters are easy to remove from the paper.

TWO-BITE BLUEBERRY MUFFINS

Makes: 24 mini muffins

Contains: Milk, Egg

Diet Type: Gluten Free

Challenge Level: Piece of Cake

Active Time: 20 minutes

Total Time: 45 minutes

INGREDIENTS

- 1½ cups **Blow Wind Blow Gluten-Free Flour Blend** (p. 71)
- 1½ teaspoons baking powder
- ¼ teaspoon baking soda
- ½ teaspoon salt
- ½ cup granulated sugar
- ¼ teaspoon ground nutmeg
- ¼ cup sour cream
- ⅓ cup applesauce
- 1 teaspoon cinnamon
- 1 stick unsalted butter, melted and cooled
- ¼ cup honey, warmed
- 1 teaspoon vanilla extract
- 1 cup blueberries
- 2 eggs, whisked

KIDS CAN

- Count the first five ingredients and sift
- Crack and whisk eggs with help
- Wash blueberries and pat dry
- Stir in blueberries

WATCH OUT FOR

- Hot oven
- Hot blueberries inside the baked muffins

INSTRUCTIONS

1. Sift together dry ingredients in a large bowl.
2. In a separate bowl combine wet ingredients: sour cream, applesauce, spices, butter, honey and vanilla.
   (***Tip:*** *Combine honey and butter in a microwave-safe bowl and heat for 30 seconds. Once cool, but still liquid, combine with other wet ingredients.*)
3. Whisk eggs and combine with other wet ingredients.
4. Pour the wet ingredients into the dry ones.
5. Stir with a fork until just incorporated.
6. Fold in the fresh blueberries.
7. Spray your mini muffin tin with cooking spray and scoop 1 tablespoon of batter into each cup.
8. Bake at 350°F for 12 minutes or until the muffins pass the "Toothpick Test."
   Repeat until you have used all the batter.
9. Allow muffins to cool before eating. Place extra muffins in a resealable plastic bag and freeze.

MOTHER GOOSE
MIX UP

Swap bananas for other fruit fillings.

BANANA GRANOLA MUFFIN CUPS

Makes: 12 granola cups	**Challenge Level:** Piece of Cake
Contains: Milk, Egg, Tree Nuts	**Active Time:** 30 minutes
Diet Type: Gluten Free	**Total Time:** 1 hour

INGREDIENTS

For the Granola Cups:

- 1½ cups oats

  (**Tip:** *Choose oats marked Gluten Free, like Bob's Red Mill*)
- 2 handfuls (½ cup) hazelnuts
- ½ teaspoon cinnamon
- ⅛ teaspoon salt
- 3 tablespoons honey
- 2 tablespoons **Nut Butter** (p. 79) or use store-bought
- 1 egg white, lightly beaten

For the Filling:

- 1 cup yogurt, more as needed
- 1 to 2 bananas, sliced

KIDS CAN

- Bash the hazelnuts
- Prepare the muffin tin with help
- Fill granola cups

WATCH OUT FOR

- Hot oven

INSTRUCTIONS

1. Place hazelnuts in a resealable plastic bag, pushing all the air out. Bash nuts with the back of a wooden spoon until broken into tiny bits.
2. Put ¼ cup of bashed nuts in a large bowl with oats, cinnamon and salt. Stir.
3. Pour the whisked egg in the oats and stir to coat.
4. Place honey and nut butter in a microwave-safe bowl and heat for 30 seconds.
5. Add the warm honey and nut butter mixture to the oats and stir until all the oats are well coated.
6. Prepare a muffin pan with cooking spray and a circle of parchment paper in the bottom of each cup.
7. Spoon 1 tablespoon of granola mixture into each muffin cup.
8. Dip fingers in water and then press the granola into the bottom of the cup. Once the bottoms are firm, go back and add granola up the sides.
9. Bake at 325°F for 30 minutes or until edges are brown
10. When granola cups are completely cool, run a knife or cake spatula around the edges and gently lift out of tin.
11. Fill cups with spoonfuls of yogurt and sliced banana. Top with remaining hazelnut bits as desired.

Nut Tree

NUT TREE

I had a little nut-tree,
Nothing would it bear
But a golden nutmeg
And a silver pear;
The King of Spain's daughter
Came to visit me,
And all for the sake
Of my little nut-tree.

Her dress was made of crimson,
Jet black was her hair,
She asked me for my nutmeg
And my golden pear.

I said, "So fair a princess
Never did I see,
I'll give you all the fruit
From my little nut-tree."

NUTRITION NIBBLE A handful of nuts each day can be a valuable addition to your child's diet. Nuts are a convenient and filling snack rich in healthy fats, fiber and protein. They contain a wide variety of vitamins, minerals and antioxidants.

PRINCESS GRANOLA

Makes:	6 to 7 cups	**Challenge Level:**	Piece of Cake
Contains:	Milk, Egg, Tree Nuts	**Active Time:**	15 minutes
Diet Type:	Gluten Free	**Total Time:**	45 minutes (includes 15 minute cooling time)

Whenever a recipe calls for chopped nuts, I call the kids. Armed with a wooden spoon and a resealable plastic bag, kids can go to town bashing nuts until they are broken into bits. It works better when everyone has their own bag so they don't end up whacking each other with the wooden spoon...and saves me time chopping.

INGREDIENTS

- 2 cups hazelnuts, chopped
- 3 cups traditional rolled oats (**Tip:** *Choose oats marked Gluten Free, like Bob's Red Mill*)
- ¼ cup honey
- ⅓ cup coconut oil
- ½ cup sliced dried pear
- ½ cup unsweetened coconut flakes
- 1 teaspoon vanilla extract
- ½ cup chocolate chips

KIDS CAN

- Bash nuts
- Measure dry ingredients
- Mix granola together
- Spread raw granola on baking sheet (subsequent stirring and spreading should be done by a parent)
- Set the timer

WATCH OUT FOR

- Hot pans and oven door
- Granola goes from golden and delicious to blackened and inedible in a flash. Keep an eye on the timer!

INSTRUCTIONS

1. Adjust oven rack to center position and preheat oven to 325°F.
   Mix all ingredients except the chocolate chips together in a large bowl.
2. Turn mixture onto a rimmed baking sheet lined with parchment paper, spreading mixture in an even layer.
3. Bake, stirring and re-spreading mixture into an even layer every 5 minutes, until granola is light golden brown, about 15 minutes.
4. Cool to room temperature.
5. Loosen dried granola with a spatula. Once cool, mix in chocolate chips and store in an airtight container.

I SAW A SHIP A'SAILING

I SAW A SHIP A'SAILING

I saw a ship a'sailing,
A'sailing on the sea.
And, oh, but it was laden
With pretty things for thee.
There were comfits in the cabin,
And apples in the hold;
The sails were made of silk
And the masts were all of gold.

The four-and-twenty sailors
That stood between the decks,
Were four-and-twenty white mice
With chains about their necks.
The captain was a duck
With a packet on his back,
And when the ship began to move
The captain said, "Quack! Quack!"

115

NUTRITION NIBBLE
Bookending each day with fruits and vegetables helps ensure your child gets the amount she needs each day. This recipe is fun to make when lots of kids are around—each person can choose the toppings for their boat and sail a spoon into their mouth. Serve this as a fancy weekend breakfast to start the day off right, or fill a huge papaya and display the ship as a beautiful and edible centerpiece for parties.

PAPAYA BOATS

Makes:	2 boats	**Challenge Level:**	Piece of Cake
Contains:	Milk, Tree Nuts	**Active Time:**	20 minutes
Diet Type:	Gluten Free	**Total Time:**	20 minutes

INGREDIENTS

- 1 medium-ripe papaya
- 1 cup plain Greek yogurt
- ½ cup fresh berries
- ½ banana, sliced
- ⅔ cup **Princess Granola** (p. 113) or substitute with a gluten-free, store-bought granola
- 1 pear, sliced
- ¼ mango, peeled and diced
- Handful dried coconut flakes to sprinkle
- Fresh mint to garnish
- Honey to drizzle
- Cinnamon to shake

KIDS CAN

- Wash and dry all fruit
- Scoop out papaya with help
- Fill the "boats"
- Sprinkle, drizzle and shake

WATCH OUT FOR

- Over-filling the papaya boats

INSTRUCTIONS

1. Wash fruit and pat dry.
2. Cut the papaya in half lengthwise. Spoon out the seeds and scrape away just a bit of the fruit to create a small boat.
3. Fill each side of the papaya equally with yogurt, fruit and granola.
4. Drizzle with honey and sprinkle with mint leaves and coconut.
5. Refrigerate for up to 24 hours.

MOTHER GOOSE MIX UP   If you can't find papayas, try making a boat with pineapple or melon.

MAN IN THE WILDERNESS

MAN IN THE WILDERNESS

The man in the wilderness asked of me,
"How many strawberries grow in the salt sea?"
I answered him, as I thought good,
As many a ship as sails in the wood.

The man in the wilderness asked me why
His hen could swim and his pig could fly.
I answered him as I thought best,
"They were both born in a cuckoo's nest."

The man in the wilderness asked me to tell
All the sands in the sea and I counted them well.
He said with a grin, "And not one more?"
I answered him, "Now you go make sure."

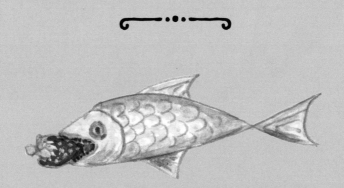

NUTRITION NIBBLE Spirulina is a type of cyanobacteria—part of a family of single-celled microbes that we often refer to as blue-green algae. It is one of the most popular supplements in the world because of its potential benefits to your body and brain. Gram for gram, spirulina may be the most nutritious food on Earth, and the amount used in this recipe is enough to reap the rewards.

SPIRULINA SMOOTHIE BOWL

Makes: 16 ounces or 1 big bowl

Contains: Milk

Diet Type: Gluten Free

Challenge Level: Piece of Cake

Active Time: 15 minutes

Total Time: 15 minutes

INGREDIENTS

- 1 cup yogurt
- ½ to 1 tablespoon blue spirulina (can substitute blue food coloring)
- 1 cup mixed seasonal fruit toppings like strawberries, figs, kiwi and goldenberries
- 1 tablespoon chia seeds

INSTRUCTIONS

1. Wash fruit and pat dry.
2. Make a yogurt "sea" by mixing blue spirulina powder and your favorite yogurt together in a bowl.
3. Decorate your smoothie bowl with fruit cut into fun shapes and finish with a sprinkle of chia seeds.

KIDS CAN

- Wash the fruit and pat dry
- Stir the yogurt and spirulina together with supervision
- Create smoothie bowl
- Sprinkle chia seeds

WATCH OUT FOR

- Blue spirulina powder can temporarily stain teeth and lips. Make sure to brush your teeth after you eat!

MOTHER GOOSE MIX UP For a tropical flare, use coconut flavored yogurt, papaya, passion or guava fruit and sliced bananas.

MAN IN THE MOON

MAN IN THE MOON

The man in the moon came down too soon
And asked the way to Norwich;
He went by the south and burnt his mouth
Eating cold plum porridge.

NUTRITION NIBBLE

Oats are among the healthiest grains—rich in carbs and fiber and higher in protein and fat than most other grains. Kids 3 to 10 years old need 8-15 grams of fiber per day. One serving of Plum Porridge meets half (4 grams) of their daily fiber needs. Juicy and antioxidant-packed spiced plums support a healthy immune system to help keep those daycare, preschool and elementary school germs at bay!

PLUM PORRIDGE

Makes: 1 to 2 cups plus plums

Contains: None of the Common Allergens

Diet Type: Gluten Free, Dairy Free

Challenge Level: Just a Pinch Involved

Active Time: 1 hour

Total Time: 1 hour

You know oatmeal is a healthy, whole grain—so how do you get your kids to eat it? Experiment with texture, temperature and taste. Creamy. Chewy. Hot. Cold. Smooth or with bits of fruit. Oats are so versatile, which is why they're scattered all throughout this cookbook.

INGREDIENTS

For the Plum Compote:
- 3 medium-ripe plums
- 1 tablespoon honey
- 2 star anise
- 1 cinnamon stick
- 4 tablespoons filtered water

For the Porridge:
- ½ cup whole oats (**Tip:** *Choose oats marked Gluten Free, like Bob's Red Mill*)
- ¾ cup almond milk
- Pinch of salt
- Seeds from ¼ vanilla pod

KIDS CAN

- Wash plums and pat dry
- Remove pit from the plums
- Smell the cinnamon and star anise
- Measure the water

WATCH OUT FOR

- Hot porridge can burn your mouth. Allow Plum Porridge to cool before serving.

INSTRUCTIONS

1. Wash and halve the plums, making sure to remove the pit. Place plums in a small saucepan with the honey, star anise, cinnamon and water.
2. Bring to a gentle simmer and turn the plums over in the cooking syrup with a spoon to coat all sides.
3. Cover with a lid and cook gently for 4 to 5 minutes until the skins are just starting to wrinkle and the plums are tender. Set plum compote aside to cool slightly while you make the porridge.
4. In a small pan, combine the oats, almond milk, vanilla seeds and salt. Heat slowly, stirring all the time, until the porridge is thick and creamy.
5. Spoon the porridge into serving bowls and top with the plum compote. Discard the cinnamon stick and star anise before serving.
6. Serve hot or cold.

MOTHER GOOSE MIX UP Sometimes we add a spoonful of coconut flavored Greek yogurt, a scattering of chopped pistachios and a little bee pollen. You can experiment with any of your own favorite toppings.

TWINKLE, TWINKLE LITTLE STAR

Twinkle, Twinkle little star

Twinkle, twinkle, little star,
How I wonder what you are,
Up above the world so high,
Like a diamond in the sky.

As your bright and tiny spark
Lights the traveler in the dark,
He would not know where to go
If you did not twinkle so.

Twinkle, twinkle, little star,
How I wonder what you are.

NUTRITION NIBBLE   In our home, breakfast is the most important meal of the day. Eating a well-balanced meal in the morning helps my children have the energy they need to play, learn and grow. Studies show that eating breakfast has a positive effect on children's cognitive performance, particularly on their memory and attention. And guess what? Grown-ups who eat breakfast get these benefits too! This dish helps busy families like yours get out the door in the morning and put their best foot forward.

CARROT CAKE OVERNIGHT OATS

Makes: 2 jars

Contains: Milk

Diet Type: Gluten Free

Challenge Level: Piece of Cake

Active Time: 30 minutes

Total Time: 8 hours (includes overnight refrigeration)

This bedtime nursery rhyme is one of the most beloved by children and parents everywhere. A simple, sweet song deserves a simple, sweet recipe that you can make in your pajamas. Stir the ingredients together and tuck your little jars of Carrot Cake Overnight Oats into a cold refrigerated bed. Enjoy in the morning with your little ones. Sweet dreams!

INGREDIENTS

- ½ cup plain Greek yogurt
- 2 tablespoons cream cheese, softened
- ½ cup rolled oats
  (**Tip:** *Choose oats marked Gluten Free, like Bob's Red Mill*)
- ⅔ cup almond milk
- 1 tablespoon chia seeds
- 1 tablespoon flax seed, whole or ground
- ½ teaspoon vanilla extract
- Pinch of salt, optional
- 1 teaspoon maple syrup
- 1 tablespoon brown sugar
- 1 large carrot, peeled and finely grated
- 4 dates, pitted and chopped
- ¼ teaspoon cinnamon
- 2 tablespoons whole milk or cream, divided and poured on top just before serving

KIDS CAN

- Measure dry ingredients
- Count the dates
- Wash the carrot
- Stir
- Screw on the jar lid

WATCH OUT FOR

- Sharp blades of the carrot grater can cut knuckles or fingers

INSTRUCTIONS

1. Before you go to bed, mix all ingredients except milk or cream together in 2 medium jars with a tight lid.
2. Refrigerate for 8 hours or overnight.
3. In the morning, open the jars, stir ingredients and top with milk or cream.
4. Enjoy directly from the jar or transfer to a small bowl.

MOTHER GOOSE MIX UP

Customization is the name of the game. You can swap in flavored Greek yogurt. Or add dried or fresh chopped tropical fruits like banana and mango. Like a little crunch? Sprinkle with 2 tablespoons of **Princess Granola** (p. 113) before serving.

GOLDEN EGG TREASURES

CAN YOU GUESS WHAT THIS RIDDLE IS DESCRIBING?

In marble walls as white as milk,
Lined with a skin as soft as silk;
Within a fountain crystal clear,
A golden apple doth appear.
No doors there are to this stronghold,
Yet thieves break in and steal the gold.

Answer: An egg.

NUTRITION NIBBLE Eggs are a great source of high-quality protein. They supply essential amino acids—the building blocks of protein—which can't be made by the body. They also provide several vitamins and minerals: vitamin A (important for healthy eyes, bones and teeth), vitamin D (also supports strong bones and teeth), choline (for brain function and heart health) and selenium (essential for thyroid function).

SKY-HIGH MUSHROOM QUICHE

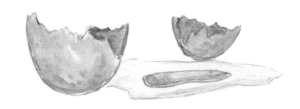

Makes: 1 quiche or 16 slices

Contains: Milk, Egg, Wheat

Challenge Level: So Worth the Effort

Active Time: 1 hour 30 minutes

Total Time: 3 hours (includes time to chill the pastry)

Using a springform pan instead of a pie plate, makes this quiche a show stopper, a jaw-dropper, an "I-can't-believe-this-didn't-come-from-a-store" type of quiche. But, it takes time and patience. The reward is impressively high walls of flaky, buttery, lightly golden crust and a deep, flavorful "meaty" (while still being vegetarian) quiche. If you're going for a quicker (albeit less impressive) option, use a pie plate instead and halve the filling recipe and the total recipe time.

INGREDIENTS

For the Pastry:

- 2½ cups all-purpose flour
- 1 teaspoon salt
- 6 tablespoons unsalted butter straight-from-the-fridge-cold
- ¾ cup (12 tablespoons) lard
- Up to 3 tablespoons cold filtered water

For the Filling:

- 1 tablespoon extra virgin olive oil
- 6 cups mushrooms, sliced (*Tip: For best results use a variety. We like portobello, shiitake, button and morel.*)
- 2 large garlic cloves, minced
- 3 purple shallots, minced
- 1 teaspoon thyme (fresh or dried)
- Salt and pepper to taste
- 12 large eggs
- 2 cups heavy cream
- 2 cups mozzarella cheese, grated
- ½ teaspoon nutmeg
- 1 teaspoon garlic powder
- 2 cups gruyere cheese, grated

KIDS CAN

- Measure dry ingredients for pastry
- Cut in butter
- Wrap pastry in plastic wrap and put in the refrigerator
- Wipe mushrooms with damp paper towel
- Crack eggs with help
- Trace the ring of the springform pan and cut a circle of parchment paper

WATCH OUT FOR

- Hot oven
- Eating raw dough is not recommended

INSTRUCTIONS ON NEXT PAGE

INSTRUCTIONS

For the Pastry:

1. In a large mixing bowl, combine flour and salt. Cut butter into cubes. Add cold cubes of butter and cut in with your fingers (a pinching motion works best) or pastry cutter.

2. Add in lard. Pinch and knead it into the pastry. Once all the fat is incorporated, add cold water 1 tablespoon at a time. Stop adding water when the pastry sticks to itself and easily forms a ball.

3. Divide the pastry into 2 balls. Wrap each in plastic wrap and put into the refrigerator for 30 minutes.

4. Remove the chilled pastry from the refrigerator and place it on a pastry mat. Flatten the ball with your hands so it resembles a large disk. Then use a rolling pin and press gently from the center out, careful not to thin out the edges. Roll pastry until it is 4 inches larger than your springform pan.

5. Place a circle of parchment paper on the bottom of the springform pan. (**Tip**: *Spray a little cooking spray underneath to help parchment stick.*)

6. Carefully roll the pastry onto the rolling pin to transfer it to the prepared pan. If the rolled pastry is too large, get a helper to lend you a hand. Allow the pastry to fall into the center of the pan and gently press the excess pastry into the walls.

7. Fortify the walls of the quiche with the pastry from the second ball. Roll out the pastry (as per step 4) and cut it into long strips. Press these strips into the existing walls of the springform pan until you have thick, sturdy walls. This step is critical for sky-high success. Trim any overhanging pastry from the top of the springform pan.

8. Place the springform pan in the refrigerator for 20 minutes so the pastry can firm up.

SKY-HIGH MUSHROOM QUICHE

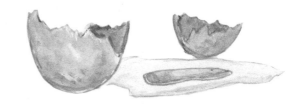

CONTINUED

INSTRUCTIONS

For the Filling:

9. In a large, nonstick frying pan, heat olive oil. Once shimmering, add garlic and shallots. Sauté for 3 minutes. Add the sliced mushrooms, thyme, salt and pepper. Cook on medium heat for 15 minutes or until mushrooms have lost their extra water and have a firm, meaty texture. Remove from heat and transfer to a bowl. Set aside to cool.

10. Combine the cream, eggs, mozzarella, ground nutmeg and garlic powder in a large bowl. Use an electric mixer to beat the mixture until frothy.

11. Preheat oven to 375° F, convection bake. Remove the springform pan from the refrigerator. Fill the springform pan with layers of mushrooms, gruyere and egg mixture until you are about two finger widths from the top of the ring.

12. Bake quiche for about 75 minutes. If you have a convection oven, start checking at 60 minutes. You'll see the quiche rise (like a soufflé) while it is in the oven, but it will fall back to be level with the pastry wall as it cools.

13. Remove from the oven when quiche is golden brown and no longer jiggles. Place it on a wire cooling rack and allow to cool completely before opening the springform pan and carefully lifting it away to reveal a perfectly sky-high quiche.

MOTHER GOOSE COOKING TIP

Give the kiddos scraps of pastry and their own rolling pin or cookie cutters to play with while you concentrate on transferring your rolled out pastry to the pan.

NUTRITION NIBBLE

There was a 6-month period when Axel wanted scrambled eggs for breakfast every day. But what about cholesterol? Is it safe to eat eggs every day? Axel is an active, growing boy, so I like including some protein at breakfast and eggs are an inexpensive, high-quality source of protein that are quick to cook. It's best to limit eggs to 1 or 2 a day, and mix it up with foods from other food groups to increase balance, and decrease picky eating in your child's diet.

WEEKDAY SCRAMBLED EGGS

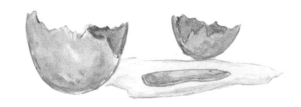

Makes: 6 eggs
Contains: Milk, Egg

Challenge Level: Piece of Cake
Active Time: 10 minutes
Total Time: 10 minutes

INGREDIENTS

- 1 tablespoon unsalted butter or ghee
- 6 eggs (or 1 egg per person)
- Optional: 1 tablespoon cream cheese (**Tip:** *This makes eggs fluffier.*)
- Seasonings to taste

KIDS CAN

- Crack the eggs
- Whisk the eggs with help

WATCH OUT FOR

- Hot stove

INSTRUCTIONS

1. Crack eggs one at a time into a large bowl.
2. Break up the yolks by piercing them with a fork and stir gently so you can still see the white and yellow part of the egg. Don't whisk.
3. In a nonstick pan, melt butter until frothy.
4. Pour eggs into the pan. Wait 1 minute, then add the cream cheese if using.
5. Stir eggs slowly but not too often, bringing in the cooked egg from the edges of the pan towards the middle.
6. Eggs are ready when they look silky. (**Tip**: *Eggs will continue to cook even after they are removed from heat*).
7. Transfer eggs to a plate and let children serve themselves.
8. Enjoy plain or sprinkle with salt, pepper, dried herbs or hot sauce.

MOTHER GOOSE MIX UP Swap **Enchilada Sauce** (p. 249) or your favorite low-sodium marinara for the aji amarillo sauce in this recipe. (***Tip**: Don't have fancy bread for croutons? Use store-bought croutons or toast sandwich bread and tear it into pieces.)*

WEEKEND BAKED EGGS

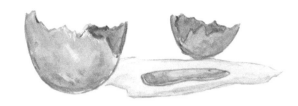

Makes: 4 cocottes

Contains: Milk, Egg, Wheat

Diet Type: Gluten Free option

Challenge Level: Just a Pinch Involved

Active Time: 45 minutes

Total Time: 1 hour

Sauces made from aji amarillo (a sweet and spicy yellow chili pepper) are a staple of Peruvian cooking that looks like captured sunshine. I think of it as the "ketchup" of Peruvian food—you can put this sauce on anything! And its medium-low heat profile tastes delicious on baked eggs. You can find aji amarillo paste in your local Latin American supermarket, some Whole Food Markets and also on Amazon.

INGREDIENTS

For the Aji Amarillo Sauce:

- 3 tablespoons aji amarillo paste (*Tip: Use more if you like it spicy*)
- 1 green onion, finely chopped
- ½ cup mayonnaise
- ¼ cup sour cream
- ½ teaspoon yellow curry powder
- 1 tablespoon ketchup
- Juice of 1 lime
- 6 saltine crackers (optional)

For the Cocotte:

- 4 ounces of your favorite bread, torn into bite sized pieces (*Tip: Use gluten-free bread to make this recipe gluten free*)
- 2 teaspoons extra virgin olive oil
- ¼ cup aji amarillo sauce
- 4 eggs (1 per cocotte)
- Salt and pepper to taste
- 4 teaspoons crumbled feta cheese (1 teaspoon per cocotte)
- 2 teaspoons chopped fresh cilantro

KIDS CAN

- Paint cocottes with oil
- Tear bread into bite sized pieces
- Crack eggs
- Wash herbs and spin dry

WATCH OUT FOR

- Hot oven
- Undercooking eggs

INSTRUCTIONS

For the Aji Amarillo Sauce:

1. Place all ingredients in blender. Mix until you obtain a smooth, yellow sauce.
2. Taste and adjust seasonings if necessary.
3. Refrigerate until you are ready to use.

For the Cocotte:

4. Preheat oven to 375°F.
5. Place bread cubes on baking sheet (to make croutons) and bake until brown and crisp, about 10 minutes.
6. Use your fingers or silicone brush to paint each cocotte with olive oil. (*Tip: Be sure to get oil up the sides*)
7. Divide bread croutons among the four cocottes.
8. Spoon 1 tablespoon of aji amarillo into each cocotte. Then crack an egg on top of the sauce.
9. Bake for 12 minutes or until whites are set. Switch oven to broil and continue to bake until yolks no longer jiggle.
10. Sprinkle each cocotte with feta crumbles and cilantro.
11. Season with salt and pepper as desired. Serve this dish "blow-on-it-hot".

GOOSEY GANDER

GOOSEY GANDER

Goosey, goosey, gander,
Whither dost thou wander?
Up stairs and down stairs,
And in my lady's chamber.

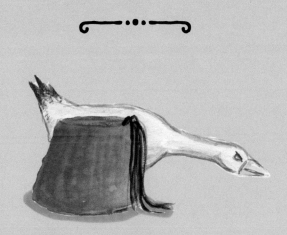

NUTRITION NIBBLE Parents are always asking me how to incorporate more vegetables into their children's diets. It's a valid question since nutrition research shows that the vast majority of children (and grown-ups) are consuming less than one serving of vegetables per day. That's a far cry from the current guidelines, which are to eat 2½ cups of vegetables throughout the day. In general, I am not a fan of hiding veggies in food. Instead, I prefer to help children learn to love veggies by serving them in surprising ways like in this chocolate banana bread.

CHOCOLATE MYSTERY BREAD (AND MUFFINS)

Makes: 1 loaf and 12 muffins or 2 loaves

Contains: Milk, Egg, Wheat

Challenge Level: Piece of Cake

Active Time: 45 minutes

Total Time: 1 hour 30 minutes

This recipe makes a lot of batter and I love a little variety when I'm baking. So, I make a single loaf and use the remaining batter for muffins. The choice is yours! Use this recipe to make two regular-sized (and delicious) loaves of Chocolate Mystery Bread or do what I do and make both muffins and a loaf.

INGREDIENTS

For the Bread:

- 1 banana
- 1 eggplant
- 1 zucchini
- 3 eggs
- ½ cup extra virgin olive oil
- 2 teaspoons vanilla extract
- ¾ cup granulated sugar
- 1 cup all-purpose flour
- 1½ cups almond flour
- 3 tablespoons natural, unsweetened cocoa powder
- ½ teaspoon baking powder
- ½ teaspoon baking soda
- ½ teaspoon salt
- ¼ teaspoon nutmeg
- ⅔ cups chocolate chips

For the Crumble:

- 4 tablespoons unsalted butter, softened to room temperature
- 2 tablespoons all-purpose flour
- ⅔ cup instant oats
- ½ cup coconut sugar or brown sugar

KIDS CAN

- Wash vegetables and pat dry
- Peel the banana
- Measure dry ingredients
- Grate vegetables with supervision
- Pinch ingredients to form a crumble
- Set a timer

WATCH OUT FOR

- Sharp edges of the grater can cut knuckles
- Hot oven
- Surprise when your kids love eggplant and zucchini

INSTRUCTIONS ON NEXT PAGE

CHOCOLATE MYSTERY BREAD (AND MUFFINS)

CONTINUED

INSTRUCTIONS

1. Preheat oven to 350°F, convection bake. Wash vegetables and pat dry. Trim the ends and then grate the zucchini and eggplant and combine in a large mixing bowl. Squeeze out some of the excess liquid from the zucchini. Peel the banana and mash it in with the vegetables.

2. In the same bowl, add eggs, olive oil, vanilla extract and sugar. Stir until combined.

3. In a separate, large mixing bowl combine the rest of the ingredients and stir until combined.

4. Make a well in the center of the dry ingredients bowl. Pour the wet ingredients into the dry ingredients and gently stir with a rubber spatula until combined. Do not overmix.

5. Prepare the bread pan by smearing the sides and bottom with butter. For muffins, prepare the muffin tin with **Artisanal Muffin Liners** (p. 105) or grease with butter.

6. Spread batter into the loaf pan(s). For muffins, spoon the batter into the muffin tin.

7. Put both in the oven and set timer for 20 minutes.

8. While the bread bakes, make the crumble. It's easy. In a small mixing bowl, pinch and mix all ingredients together until it forms a crumbly dough.

9. When timer sounds, remove the bread and muffins from the oven and gently press the crumble in on top. (**Tip**: *If you add the crumble before baking, it sinks to the bottom.*)

10. Cover the bread loosely with aluminum foil. Return both the covered bread and uncovered muffins to the oven.

11. Set a muffin timer for 10 minutes and a bread timer for 30 minutes. When timers sound, do the "Toothpick Test."

12. Allow bread and muffins to cool before removing from their pans and serving. (**Tip**: *The finished product freezes well.*)

SIPPITY SUP

SIPPITY SUP

Sippity sup, sippity sup,
Bread and milk from a china cup.
Bread and milk from a bright silver spoon
Made of a piece of the bright silver moon.
Sippity sup, sippity sup,
Sippity, sippity sup.

MOTHER GOOSE MIX UP

Personalize spoonbread by adding pulled pork (see recipe for **Tom's Pulled Pork** on p. 321), chopped onions, grated cheese or honey into the "mush" before baking.

SILVER SPOONBREAD

Makes: 6 cups

Contains: Milk, Egg, Wheat

Challenge Level: Piece of Cake

Active Time: 25 minutes

Total Time: 1 hour

Spoonbread is kind of like a cornbread soufflé with a history that dates back to Native American cultures. I adapted this basic recipe from my Gran, a strong southern woman who was also part Cherokee Indian. She inherited the recipe from her mom, my Great Grandma Lacey. I lived with my Gran for years on her farm in Alabama. Gran wasn't a great chef—she had other talents like riding horses and sewing. But the exception was her stellar spoonbread—smooth and soft with a few handfuls of sweet corn for texture. Versatile is this dish's middle name. Spoonbread's neutral, creamy base can be adapted to sweet or savory palettes (see the Mother Goose Mix Ups) or enjoyed in its classic form. Give a spoon to everyone at the table and let family and friends help themselves directly from the hot skillet.

INGREDIENTS

- ⅓ cup cornmeal
- 4 cups milk
- 4 tablespoons unsalted butter
- 1 to 2 handfuls fresh or frozen corn
- 3 eggs
- 2 tablespoons all-purpose flour
- ½ teaspoon salt

KIDS CAN

- Crack and whisk eggs with help
- Count cups of milk

WATCH OUT FOR

- Hot oven

INSTRUCTIONS

1. Preheat oven to 350°F, convection bake.
2. Heat a large saucepan on the stove and add the milk.
3. Sprinkle cornmeal over milk and bring to a boil. Stir often and gently until slightly thickened, about 15 minutes.
4. Using part of the butter, liberally grease the bottom and sides of a cast iron skillet.
5. Drop the rest of the butter into the thickened batter to melt. Stir in the corn.
6. In a separate bowl, beat eggs until very thick and fluffy.
7. Combine the flour and salt.
8. Add the eggs, flour and salt to the saucepan. Stir to combine and turn off the stove.
9. Transfer the liquid batter into the skillet and bake for 35 minutes until puffed and golden. (***Tip:*** *If you don't have a convection oven, switch heat to broil and bake for another 3 to 5 minutes until the top is golden.*)

The Queen of Hearts

THE QUEEN OF HEARTS

The Queen of Hearts,
She made some tarts
All on a summer's day.

The Knave of Hearts,
He stole the tarts
And took them clean away.

The King of Hearts,
Called for the tarts
And beat the Knave full sore.

The Knave of Hearts,
Brought back the tarts
And vowed he'd steal no more.

NUTRITION NIBBLE What better way to energize your morning than with a homemade breakfast tart filled with fresh berries! High in antioxidants and fiber and big on flavor, tiny berries might be the world's most perfect fruit. Good morning, sunshine!

HEART TARTS

Makes: 10 to 12 tarts
Contains: Milk, Wheat

Challenge Level: Just a Pinch Involved
Active Time: 1 hour
Total Time: 2 hours 15 minutes (includes resting time)

My in-laws live in Portland, Oregon and we go to visit them every summer. One of our traditions is to go to Sauvie's Island, a little farming community full of U-Pick berry farms. The kids love to pick and taste berries as we fill our baskets. There is nothing tastier than a slightly tart, sun-ripened berry that you pick yourself and eat right there on the farm. While my favorite way to enjoy raspberries, blueberries and blackberries is rinsed and whole, we also set some aside to make these delicious heart tarts.

INGREDIENTS

For the Dough:
- 2½ cups all-purpose flour
- 2 tablespoons granulated sugar
- 1 teaspoon salt
- 14 tablespoons (1 stick plus 6 tablespoons) unsalted butter, straight-from-the-fridge-cold
- 3 tablespoons milk plus more to paint the tarts before they go in the oven

For the Marmalade:
- 3 cups berries (I used a mix of raspberries, blueberries and blackberries)
- ¾ cup granulated sugar
- Juice of half a lemon or 1 tablespoon champagne vinegar

For the Glaze:
- ⅔ cup powdered sugar
- Milk as needed (I use about 1½ tablespoons)
- Freeze dried raspberries or sprinkles

KIDS CAN

- Cut in butter
- Mix dough with their hands
- Squeeze the lemon for juice
- Use the cookie cutter
- Paint borders with milk
- Decorate

WATCH OUT FOR

- Hot oven
- Sticky fingers on your furniture

INSTRUCTIONS ON NEXT PAGE

INSTRUCTIONS

For the Dough:

1. Chop the butter into cubes and mix it in a bowl with the flour, sugar and salt.
2. Use your fingers to cut in the butter (use a pinching motion) with the dry ingredients until there are no chunks of butter left and your mix looks like breadcrumbs. *(**Tip:** You can also add dry ingredients to a food processor and drop cubes of butter into the moving mixer. Pulse until incorporated.)*
3. Add the milk and mix using your hands. *(**Tip:** You can also do this step in a food processor.)*
4. Wrap the dough in plastic wrap and let it rest in the fridge for 20 minutes. If you forget about it and leave it in there longer, don't worry. Just let the dough come to room temperature before rolling it.

HEART TARTS CONTINUED

INSTRUCTIONS

For the Marmalade:

5. Place all the ingredients in a pot and let it cook until it looks like runny marmalade.

6. Let marmalade cool completely. Once cooled, it will double in thickness. If it is too thick, you can add a bit more lemon juice or water. (**Tip:** *If you only use raspberries, the marmalade will be even thicker because of the pectin present in the seeds.*)

For the Assembly:

7. Preheat oven to 350°F.

8. Roll the dough until it's ⅛ inch (2mm) thick. It's best if you roll one half of the dough at a time. If dough gets too soft, put it back in the fridge to firm up.

9. Use a heart-shaped cookie cutter to make heart shapes or cut the dough into rectangles a little bigger than the palm of your child's hand.

10. Place the hearts on a baking tray lined with a silpat or parchment paper and plop a generous tablespoon of marmalade in the center of each heart, smearing it slightly with the back of the spoon. Leave a decent border around the edge.

11. Paint the border with milk and place another piece of dough on top. Press down on the edges with your fingers to seal the top and bottom and then gently press the edges with the tip of a fork to make the edges look pretty.

12. Use a toothpick to make 3 diagonal holes on the top of the tart so the steam from the marmalade can escape.

13. Paint the heart tarts with milk and bake for 15 minutes or until lightly golden.

For the Glaze:

14. Make sure the tarts have completely cooled off before making the glaze or it will melt and run off.

15. Place powdered sugar in a bowl and add milk little by little. Whisk together, and stop adding milk once you have a thick, white glaze.

16. Use a teaspoon to pour glaze on top of your heart starting in the middle. Use the back of the teaspoon to spread the glaze to the edges.

17. Garnish with freeze-dried raspberries or sprinkles. (**Tip:** *You can reuse the dough that's left behind after the hearts are cut to make cookies. If the dough feels a little dry, add a few drops of water to bring it back to life.*)

THE MULBERRY BUSH

The Mulberry Bush

Here we go 'round the mulberry bush,
The mulberry bush, the mulberry bush.
Here we go 'round the mulberry bush,
On a cold and frosty morning.

REAL VANILLA EXTRACT
(AS OPPOSED TO IMITATION VANILLA)
IS WORTH THE EXTRA MONEY.
IT HAS A DEPTH OF FLAVOR THAT
ENHANCES WHATEVER YOU'RE
MAKING. WE LIKE MCCORMICK
PURE VANILLA EXTRACT FOR ITS
FLAVOR AND QUALITY.

NUTRITION NIBBLE

You probably didn't expect to find donuts in a nutritionist's cookbook! Remember, a balanced diet makes room for all kinds of food and these mini donuts are the perfect portions of sweetness for you and your family. So, go ahead and have a donut morning every now and then.

CAKE DONUTS ⟨WITH⟩ MULBERRY GLAZE

Makes: 12 mini donuts

Contains: Milk, Egg

Diet Type: Gluten Free

Challenge Level: Piece of Cake

Active Time: 30 minutes

Total Time: 30 minutes

Note: I used Babycakes mini donut maker. You can also bake donuts in the oven using a silicone donut mold.

INGREDIENTS

For the Donuts:
- 1 cup **Blow Wind Blow Gluten-Free Flour Blend** (p. 71)
- ½ teaspoon baking soda
- ¼ teaspoon nutmeg
- 1 tablespoon mulberry jam
- 1 egg
- ½ teaspoon vanilla extract
- ½ cup sour cream (can substitute plain Greek yogurt)
- ¼ cup vegetable oil
- ½ cup granulated sugar

For the Mulberry Glaze:
- 1 cup powdered sugar
- ½ tablespoon mulberry jam
- ¼ cup unsalted butter, melted
- ¼ teaspoon vanilla extract
- 2 tablespoons hot filtered water

KIDS CAN

- Stir dough
- Dip donuts in mulberry glaze
- Lick fingers

WATCH OUT FOR

- Being woken up long before you are ready to make donuts with your child on a cold and frosty Saturday morning

INSTRUCTIONS

1. Set a wire cooling rack on top of parchment paper or baking sheet. Set aside.
2. Make the donut dough. Stir together gluten-free flour, baking soda and nutmeg in a large bowl. Set aside. In a small bowl, combine and whisk together the rest of the donut ingredients.
3. Plug in the donut maker so it preheats. If using a silicone donut mold, preheat oven to 350°F.
4. Transfer the donut dough to a piping bag (normally used for frosting) with a wide mouth. Squeeze and fill the donut spaces in the donut maker (or fill your silicone mold). Close the donut maker and set a timer for 4 minutes. Oven-baked donuts will take longer, 10 to 12 minutes.
5. Meanwhile, stir together all the glaze ingredients in a bowl and set aside.
6. Transfer baked donuts to a wire rack to cool. Refill the donut maker and continue until all the donuts are baked.
7. Once donuts are cool, dip them in the glaze. Be sure to dip both sides. If your glaze becomes hard, warm it in the microwave. For an extra sweet treat, dip donuts twice.

HANDY PANDY

HANDY PANDY

Handy Pandy, Jack a dandy
Loves plum cake and sugar candy.
He bought some at a grocer's shop
And out he came, hop, hop, hop!

This cake gets its moist and dense flavor from the yogurt
and its gorgeous color from plums. It works well as a
special occasion breakfast cake or as a dessert.

This is my substitute for Axel's favorite: Starbucks lemon cake.
The best part? It still goes great with my skinny vanilla latte.

NUTRITION NIBBLE Plums contain polyphenols, which help "keep things moving" and improve digestion, but most of you already know that. This cake recipe uses olive oil, a heart-healthy unsaturated fat. The majority of the fat in olive oil is a monounsaturated fat called oleic acid. Studies show that oleic acid reduces inflammation and may even reduce cancer risk. Recipes in this book use extra virgin olive oil whenever possible as the fat of choice. That way, even sweets can have some nutritional benefits!

YOGURT PLUMCAKE with PLUM GLAZE

Makes:	1 cake or 10 slices	**Challenge Level:**	Just a Pinch Involved
Contains:	Milk, Egg	**Active Time:**	40 minutes
Diet Type:	Gluten Free	**Total Time:**	1 hour 15 minutes

INGREDIENTS

For the Cake:

- 1 cup **Blow Wind Blow Gluten-Free Flour Blend** (p. 71)
- ½ cup tapioca starch or ¼ cup corn starch
- 7 ounces peach yogurt at room temperature
- 3 eggs
- ¾ cup granulated sugar
- 7 tablespoons extra virgin oil
- 1 teaspoon vanilla extract
- Zest of 1 lemon or small orange
- 1 teaspoon baking powder
- Pinch of salt

For the Glaze:

- 3 plums cut in half and pitted
- ½ cup brown sugar
- Pinch of ground cloves
- Pinch of cinnamon
- Pinch of nutmeg
- ⅔ cup powdered sugar
- 1 tablespoon cream cheese
- 1 tablespoon unsalted butter
- 2 tablespoons milk

KIDS CAN

- Sift flour and starch
- Bathe yogurt
- Wash plums and pat dry
- Mix the brown sugar and spices
- Prepare the plumcake baking dish with cooking spray and flour

WATCH OUT FOR

- Hot oven

INSTRUCTIONS ON NEXT PAGE

163

YOGURT PLUMCAKE PLUM GLAZE

CONTINUED

INSTRUCTIONS

1. Preheat oven to 340°F, convection bake.

2. Bring yogurt to room temperature. Place yogurt in a bowl of warm water—pretend your yogurt is taking a bath! This step is super important because the cake will not rise if the yogurt is cold. To test, bring yogurt to your lips. If it is cold, return it to the warm bath.

3. Sift tapioca starch, baking powder and flour together.

4. In a separate bowl or in a stand-up mixer, beat the eggs, sugar, salt, vanilla and zest until frothy, soft and clear. About 5 minutes.

5. Slowly add oil while continuing to beat the mixture.

6. Add two tablespoons of the sifted dry ingredients into the egg mixture.

7. Continue to whisk at low speed as you add the yogurt, a couple of spoonfuls at a time.

8. Incorporate the rest of the flour into the batter.

9. Prepare your silicone cake pan or bread pan with cooking spray and a light dusting of flour.

10. Pour batter into the cake pan.

11. In a separate oven safe dish, combine plums with brown sugar and spices.

12. Bake plums alongside the plum cake for 40 minutes. Do not open the oven during this time or the plum cake will fall.

13. When the plumcake passes "Toothpick Test" it is ready. Set plumcake on a wire rack to cool in its pan.

14. With the back of a fork, mash the cooked plums until no longer lumpy.

15. Cream butter, cream cheese and powdered sugar together. Add milk and mashed plums to make the glaze. (**Tip:** *If glaze is too thick to pour, add 1 to 2 tablespoons milk to reach desired consistency.*)

16. When cake has cooled, remove from pan and cover with the glaze.

17. Serve at room temperature or chilled.

165

WHAT ARE LITTLE KIDS MADE OF?

What Are Little Boys Made Of?

What are little boys made of?
Snips and snails
And puppy-dogs' tails,
That's what little boys are made of.

— ··· —

What Are Little Girls Made Of?

What are little girls made of?
Sugar and spice
And everything nice,
That's what little girls are made of.

NUTRITION NIBBLE Great for a quick breakfast, energy balls also make a perfect no-bake snack. They are fun to make, especially when taking on a "tail" form. Your kids will wag and wiggle like a sweet puppy, fully energized by a high protein, healthy fat, fiber-filled snack. For extra laughs, we like to listen to the kid-friendly version of "Who Let the Dogs Out" as we roll these puppies in cinnamon, cocoa powder and coconut flakes, "Woof, woof, woof, woof, woof!"

PUPPY DOG TAILS

Makes: 12 "tails"

Contains: Tree nuts, Peanuts

Diet Type: Gluten Free, Dairy Free

Challenge Level: Piece of Cake

Active Time: 15 minutes

Total Time: 20 minutes

INGREDIENTS

- 1 cup unsalted, roasted nuts
  (a mix of your favorite works best)
- 1 cup dates, pitted and chopped
- 2 tablespoons honey
- 1 teaspoon vanilla extract
- Pinch of salt
- Cinnamon, cocoa powder, chocolate sprinkles
  or coconut flakes

KIDS CAN

- Add the ingredients to the food processor
- Push the button of the food processor
  with supervision
- Form tails and roll in different toppings

WATCH OUT FOR

- Sharp blades of the food processor

INSTRUCTIONS

1. Mix dates, nuts, honey, vanilla and salt in a food processor. If necessary, add a teaspoon of hot water to help your food processor blend the ingredients—I don't recommend more than that or the mixture is too soft to roll.
2. Spray your hands with cooking spray or moisten them with water and roll the mixture into "tails" using about 1 tablespoon of mix per "tail."
3. Pour cinnamon, cocoa, coconut or chocolate sprinkles on individual plates.
4. Gently roll the puppy dog "tail" in the toppings to change its color and enhance it's flavor.
5. Place "tails" in the refrigerator to firm up for at least 5 minutes before eating.
6. Store extra "tails" in the refrigerator or freeze on the day of preparation.

CINNAMON ROLLS

Makes: 12 rolls	**Challenge Level:** Just a Pinch Involved
Contains: Milk, Egg, Wheat	**Active Time:** 30 minutes
	Total Time: 2 hours (yeast needs 1 hour to rise)

INGREDIENTS

For the Filling: Just combine the ingredients in a medium bowl and stir until smooth.

- 1 cup **Apple Butter** (p. 81) or use store-bought
- 6 tablespoons granulated sugar
- 1 tablespoon cinnamon
- ¾ teaspoon ginger
- ½ teaspoon paprika
- ¼ teaspoon nutmeg

    Note: If icing rolls, set aside 1 tablespoon of the filling

For the Dough:
- 4 cups all-purpose flour
- 1½ teaspoons salt
- 2¼ teaspoons instant dry yeast
- ½ cup granulated sugar
- 1 cup milk at room temperature
- ⅓ cup unsalted melted butter cooled to room temperature
- 1 egg at room temperature
- ½ teaspoon vanilla extract

KIDS CAN

- Stir together the spice blend
- Measure dry ingredients
- Flour the surface of a table or rolling mat
- Use the rolling pin
- Spread the filling
- Set the timer

WATCH OUT FOR

- Sharp knife that cuts the log into individual rolls
- Hot oven door

INSTRUCTIONS ON NEXT PAGE

MOTHER GOOSE MIX UP

We almost never add icing to our cinnamon rolls as they are sweet, gooey and oh-so-yummy already. However, if you choose to frost them, add a splash of milk to the icing and pour it over the rolls while they are still hot. This way, the icing can seep into all the nooks and crannies (like a glaze) and you don't tear your roll trying to spread icing on with a knife.

SUGAR AND SPICE ICING (OPTIONAL)

Makes: ½ cup icing

Contains: Milk

Diet Type: Gluten Free

When cinnamon rolls are finished, remove from oven and allow to cool for 5 minutes before icing them. Serve warm, room temperature or cold (*Tip: You can freeze rolls for future breakfasts or treats!*)

INGREDIENTS AND INSTRUCTIONS

This one's easy! Just mix the following ingredients together in a bowl and pour over warm rolls.

- 1 tablespoon reserved filling
- ⅔ cup powdered sugar
- 1½ tablespoons milk to make an icing thin enough to pour

CINNAMON ROLLS   CONTINUED

INSTRUCTIONS

For the Dough:

1. Mix together the wet ingredients: milk, egg, vanilla and melted butter.

2. Mix all dry ingredients (including the yeast) in a separate bowl. Make a hole or well in the center and add all the wet ingredients to the center of the dry ingredients.

3. Stir until you have a uniform dough. It's really sticky—don't worry, the stickiness makes the rolls gooey instead of bready and hard.

4. Let the dough rest for 1 hour covered in plastic wrap or until it doubles in size.
   (***Tip:*** *If it's too cold in your house, turn on your oven until it's warm, but not too hot inside, and let the dough puff up in there.*)

To Assemble the Cinnamon Rolls:

5. Prepare a large, flat surface with flour or a rolling mat sprinkled with flour. Also flour your hands and the rolling pin.

6. Roll out the dough to roughly a 10 x 12 inch rectangle, ¼ inch thick.
   If it's too sticky, sprinkle the dough with more flour.

7. Spread a smooth, thin layer of filling all over the dough.

8. Turn the rectangle so the long side is facing you. With two hands, from the long side, slowly and carefully begin rolling the dough. Your first two rolls should be small and tight. These will be the center of the cinnamon roll.

9. Continue to roll until you get to the other end.

10. Press the edges of the dough together so it sticks to itself and you have a nice even log.
    If you get a tear, just mend it by pinching the dough together.

11. Cut the log into individual rolls about the width of 3 fingers side by side.
    If the dough is unrolling, place it in the freezer for 10 minutes to firm it up.

12. Prepare your baking dish with parchment paper. Place the cinnamon rolls inside and space them evenly apart. The rolls will grow to fill in the space.

13. Bake at 375°F, convection bake, for 20 to 30 minutes, depending on your oven.

14. Prepare your icing (optional) while the rolls are baking.

CHAPTER 3

Slurpy Soups

Homemade soups are filling, hydrating and an innovative way to make leftover ingredients taste like new. Plus, homemade soup is another opportunity to increase vegetable intake. I didn't think my kids would get "into" soup, but I was wrong. They like the challenge of slurping broth on a spoon and the comedy of shoveling sturdier soups like **Savory Lentil Stew** (p. 191) into their mouth.

There really is a soup for every occasion; they aren't just for sick days (although **Team Chicken Soup** (p. 181) always perks us up when we feel under the weather)! On hot days make **Pea and Avocado Gazpacho** (p. 199). In a rush? Make **Egg Drop Soup** (p. 187), for a quick meal that takes just minutes.

Before you get started, here's a quick shout out to a few scrumptious soups that are "living" in other chapters—I kept these soups with the rhymes that inspired them. Go to page 63 for **Vegetable Broth and Other Stocks,** page 361 for **Moqueca Stew with Salmon**, and flip to page 269 to find my **Potato Soup** recipe!

FI! FIE! FOE! FUM!

FI! FIE! FOE! FUM!

Fi! Fie! Foe! Fum!
I smell the blood of an Englishman.
Be he 'live or be he dead,
I'll grind his bones to make my bread.

—···—

SOUPS FOR GIANT APPETITES

Are you really hungry? Good!
These soups satisfy even GIANT appetites!

P.S. No Englishmen were harmed in the following recipes...

NOTE: IF YOU DON'T HAVE FISH STOCK, SUBSTITUTE WITH AN EQUAL AMOUNT OF CHICKEN OR VEGETABLE BROTH PLUS 1 TEASPOON FISH SAUCE.

NUTRITION NIBBLE Nourishing broth and mollusks packed with vitamins and minerals (iron, zinc, phosphorus, magnesium and B12) power up this flavorful and vibrant soup. It's a great introduction to the more "exotic" frutti di mare.

SEAFOOD SOUP

Makes:	12 cups (includes shells)	**Challenge Level:**	Just a Pinch Involved
Contains:	Shellfish, Fish	**Active Time:**	1 hour
Diet Type:	Gluten Free, Dairy Free	**Total Time:**	1 hour

This Italian-American soup has a richly flavored broth and holds a ton of seafood without being heavy. Tasty morsels of fish, shellfish and squid make this a "play with your food" kind of meal. My kids love salmon, so I use it as the base and layer flavors from there. Axel and Rex usually ask for more mussels so they can use the shells to scoop the broth. As they love to say: "Mussels give us big muscles!"

INGREDIENTS

- 3 tablespoons extra virgin olive oil
- 3 shallots, diced
- 1 fennel bulb, thinly sliced (save leaves for garnish)
- ½ cup celery, sliced into thin half moons
- 1 cup carrot, peeled and diced
- 3 cloves garlic, minced
- 1 teaspoon salt
- ½ teaspoon black pepper
- ¼ teaspoon red pepper flakes, or to taste
- ¼ cup tomato paste

- 2 cups canned diced tomatoes in juice
- 1½ cups dry white wine
- 6 cups **Fish Stock** (p. 67) or see **Note** on left
- 1 pound fresh live clams
- 1 pound fresh live mussels, cleaned and debearded
- 12 fresh scallops
- 1 pound skinless salmon, cut into 2 inch chunks
- ½ pound (8 ounces) frozen squid rings, defrosted and drained

INSTRUCTIONS

1. Place a large heavy-bottomed pot or dutch oven over medium heat on the stove.
2. Add olive oil. When it starts to shimmer, add the shallots and fennel. Sauté for 5 minutes.
3. Add celery, carrots and garlic. Sauté for 5 minutes.
4. Add salt, pepper and chili flakes, stir. Immediately add tomato paste. Cook, stirring constantly for 1 minute.
5. Pour in the canned tomatoes and wine. Cook for 15 minutes until wine reduces by half.

6. Add the fish stock. Cook for 20 minutes.
7. Get a spoonful of soup with carrot and celery. Allow it to cool and then taste. If veggies are tender, add shellfish.
8. Cook clams and mussels for 5 minutes then add the rest of the seafood (salmon, squid and scallops). Cook for another 5 minutes then turn off heat.
9. Set the table and serve soup with your favorite artisanal bread.

KIDS CAN
- Wash produce and pat dry
- Clean and debeard mussels
- Clean clams in clean water
- Count cups of fish stock

WATCH OUT FOR
- Wash hands after handling seafood
- Hot stove
- Sharp knives

TEAM CHICKEN SOUP

Makes: 9 cups

Contains: Milk, Wheat

Challenge Level: Just a Pinch Involved

Active Time: 45 minutes

Total Time: 1 hour

On one of the last photoshoots for this cookbook, Axel announced he wanted chicken soup for dinner. I responded, "sorry dude, we are eating food from the photoshoot tonight. We can make chicken soup another time." Axel countered, "What if you take some pictures of chicken soup because I love it!" He asked Rex, "Hey, are you on my team?". Rex responded, "I'm on Team Chicken Soup!" I know I told you when your kid asks for something that's not on the menu, "stand your ground" (for a refresher see p. 24). But, well, err—maybe the cookbook wouldn't be complete without "Team Chicken Soup." So, I whipped it up, Lorena took the photo, and there you are!

INGREDIENTS

- 2 tablespoons unsalted butter
- 2 tablespoons extra virgin olive oil, divided
- 1 cup sliced baby portobello mushrooms
- 2 tablespoons all-purpose flour
- 1 tablespoon dried garlic flakes
- 1 tablespoon dried marjoram
- 1 tablespoon dried basil
- 6 cups **Chicken Stock** (p. 63) or store-bought option, divided
- 2 medium-sized zucchini, thinly sliced
- 12 ounces boneless, skinless chicken breasts
- 1 carrot, grated
- 2 green onions, thinly sliced
- Handful fresh parsley, minced
- Handful fresh basil, minced
- 1 cup baby spinach, chopped
- ¼ teaspoon salt
- ¼ teaspoon pepper
- 3 leaves chard, deveined and cut chiffonade

KIDS CAN

- Wash produce and pat dry
- Wash leaves and spin dry
- Count cups of chicken stock

WATCH OUT FOR

- Hot stove and hot soup
- Making this soup when you weren't planning to

INSTRUCTIONS ON NEXT PAGE

TO MAKE THESE
TWO-BITE
BLUEBERRY MUFFINS
TURN TO PAGE 107

MOTHER GOOSE
MIX UP   For a heartier soup, add noodles or canned chickpeas (make sure to rinse
and drain the chickpeas first).

TEAM CHICKEN SOUP CONTINUED

P.S. Axel and Rex (the master negotiators on the left) did end up eating chicken soup for dinner and the food from the photoshoot (like these **Two-Bite Blueberry Muffins**). More proof that, when kids listen to their bodies and we listen to them, good things happen!

INSTRUCTIONS

For the Mushrooms:

1. In a large nonstick frying pan, heat butter and 1 tablespoon olive oil over medium heat.
2. Add mushrooms and sauté until mushrooms are tender, about 5 minutes.
3. Whisk flour with the dried garlic, marjoram and basil into 1 cup of chicken stock.
4. Add stock to the mushrooms and cook, stirring occasionally, until liquid reduces by half (about 15 minutes).
5. When mushrooms have reduced, transfer to a bowl. Return the frying pan to the stove.

While the Mushroom and Stock Reduce, Boil the Chicken:

6. Partially fill a deep pot with water and bring to a boil. Place chicken breasts inside and boil until cooked through. This usually takes 20 minutes.
7. Drain water and set chicken aside to cool. Once cool, use two forks to shred chicken.

For the Rest of the Veggies:

8. Add remaining 1 tablespoon of olive oil to the frying pan. Set the stove to medium heat.
9. Sauté shredded carrots and green onion for 5 minutes, then add zucchini and sauté 5 minutes more.
10. Add fresh herbs, spinach, salt and pepper.
11. When veggies are tender and spinach has wilted, remove from heat.
12. In a large pot, warm the remaining chicken stock.
13. Add the mushrooms, veggies, chicken and finally, the fresh chard to the pot.
14. Serve warm.

HUMPTY DUMPTY

HUMPTY DUMPTY

Humpty Dumpty sat on a wall,
Humpty Dumpty had a great fall;
All the King's horses and all the King's men
Couldn't put Humpty together again.

What could we make when Humpty Dumpty falls off the wall and breaks to pieces? Egg Drop Soup, of course! This recipe is fast and easy to whip up on sick days, as a post-exercise snack or when you don't have much in the way of ingredients. This nutritious soup will put you back together again!

NUTRITION NIBBLE Flavorful and nourishing **Chicken Stock** (p. 63) and high quality egg protein make this a gentle, healing meal. Stock contains nutrients, as well as collagen, marrow, amino acids and minerals, which help protect the digestive tract, improve sleep and support joint health.

EGG DROP SOUP

Makes: 6 cups
Contains: Egg, Wheat
Diet Type: Gluten Free, Dairy Free Option

Challenge Level: Piece of Cake
Active Time: 10 minutes
Total Time: 10 minutes

INGREDIENTS

- 1 tablespoon butter, ghee or lard
- 6 cups **Chicken Stock** (p. 63) or your favorite store-bought option
- 1 garlic clove, minced
- 6 eggs, whisked (**Tip**: *Use 1 egg per person*)
- 2 spoonfuls salsa of your choice
- Splash of your favorite hot sauce, optional (we like Frank's Hot Sauce)
- Fresh chives, for garnish

KIDS CAN

- Crack and whisk the eggs with help
- Count the cups of broth as you add them to the pot

WATCH OUT FOR

- Hot stove and boiling broth
- This is a fast recipe. Be ready with your bowls!

INSTRUCTIONS

1. In a large pot add garlic and ghee. Sauté for 2 minutes.
2. Add broth and bring everything to a low boil.
3. In a separate bowl, whisk eggs.
4. When the broth starts to boil, turn off the heat.
5. Pour eggs into hot broth and stir rapidly.
6. Spoon in the salsa.
7. Garnish with fresh chopped chives, hot sauce, salt and pepper as desired.
8. Serve immediately or "blow-on-it-hot".

MOTHER GOOSE MIX UP
If you want a little more "oomph" add rice noodles to this soup before serving. Rice noodles, also called vermicelli, cook quickly (about 2 minutes, see the package instructions) and are gluten free.

WITCHES BREW

WITCHES BREW

Witches brew make me a stew.
Don't make it thick else I'll be sick.
Make enough for the week ahead,
And hurry up it's time for bed.

Chileans eat lentils and grapes and wear yellow underwear on New Year's Eve for good luck. The first time I introduced these traditions to Axel and Rex, they were quite keen to don yellow underpants and eat grapes, but were decidedly less gung-ho as they looked at the bowl of Savory Lentil Stew. It's true lentils aren't very attractive, but I warned them not to judge the tastiness of this dish solely on appearance. Plus, the boys only needed to take one tiny taste to guarantee good luck. You may not believe it, but we did get lucky. Axel and Rex discovered a new favorite dish! I make these lentils once a month, and freeze extras for a babysitter to pull out and reheat. The kids can have a protein and veggie-packed meal on the table as quick as you can say "defrost!" and I get to have a date night with my husband.

NUTRITION NIBBLE

Lentils are often overlooked because of their mushy, greenish-brown appearance. Don't let that be the case in your home! Classified by their color, this legume is high in plant-based protein, iron and fiber, making them a perfect meat alternative. Lentils are also chock full of magnesium, zinc, potassium and B vitamins, all of which help the body run properly. Green on the outside is good on the inside.

SAVORY LENTIL STEW

Makes: About 4 cups

Contains: None of the Common Allergens

Diet Type: Gluten Free, Dairy Free

Challenge Level: Just a Pinch Involved

Active Time: 45 minutes

Total Time: 1 hour

INGREDIENTS

- 8 cups **Chicken Stock** (p. 63) or any store-bought option, divided (**Tip**: *You can use vegetable broth*)
- 1½ cups green lentils
- 1 to 2 tablespoons extra virgin olive oil
- 1 purple onion
- 4 stalks of Swiss chard (leaf and stem)
- 1 handful fresh parsley
- 2 carrots
- 2 tomatoes
- 2 to 3 green onions, sliced thin

KIDS CAN

- Wash and dry produce
- Measure and rinse lentils
- Count cups of broth as you pour
- Set the timer

WATCH OUT FOR

- Hot stove
- Knives chopping vegetables

INSTRUCTIONS

1. Add 4 cups of stock to a large lidded pot and set heat to high.
2. While stock warms, rinse the lentils. Add lentils, and when the stock starts to boil, cover it and reduce the heat to medium.
3. Lentils will take 45 to 60 minutes to cook. Set a timer for 45 minutes. Check lentils every 10 minutes to top up with more stock. Expect to add up to 4 cups more stock during the cooking process.
4. Roughly chop chard and parsley, dice the purple onion, grate the carrots, slice the green onion, and chop the tomatoes into cubes.
5. Place a skillet on medium heat and add enough olive oil to coat the bottom.
6. Once warm, add the onions and sauté for 5 to 7 minutes. When they become soft, add in the swiss chard and parsley.
7. When the leaves are wilted, add the carrots and tomatoes.
8. Allow to cook, stirring occasionally until you have a fragrant sofrito, about 10 minutes more.
9. When the 45-minute timer sounds check on the lentils. If the lentils are soft, reduce the heat and add the sofrito. Cook everything together so the flavors combine. If the lentils are still hard, add a bit of water and continue to simmer. Once soft, proceed as above. Serve warm.

PEAS PORRIDGE HOT, PEAS PORRIDGE COLD

PEAS PORRIDGE HOT, PEAS PORRIDGE COLD

Peas porridge hot, peas porridge cold,

Peas porridge in the pot, nine days old;

Some like it hot, some like it cold,

Some like it in the pot, nine days old.

Before jumping into cooking,

Play the "Peas Porridge Hot" game with your little.

See the photos and instructions on the next page.

PEAS PORRIDGE HOT, PEAS PORRIDGE COLD

Peas (clap hands to thighs) **porridge** (clap own hands together) **hot** (clap friend's hands),

Peas (clap hands to thighs) **porridge** (clap own hands together) **cold** (clap friend's hands),

Peas porridge hot, peas porridge cold,
Peas porridge in the pot, nine days old;
Some like it hot, some like it cold,
Some like it in the pot, nine days old.

Peas (clap hands to thighs) **porridge** (clap own hands together) **in the** (clap right hands only) **pot** (clap own hands),

Nine (clap left hands only) **days** (clap own hands) **old** (clap partner's hands).

NUTRITION
NIBBLE

Garden peas are a popular food all around the world. Did you know, peas are not a vegetable at all, peas are a legume! Lentils, chickpeas, beans and peanuts are also legumes. Like most legumes, peas are high in complex carbs (think starch and fiber) and an excellent source of plant-based protein, which is a major reason why this recipe is so filling.

PEA, PROSCIUTTO AND MINT RISOTTO

Makes: 6 cups

Contains: Milk

Diet Type: Gluten Free

Challenge Level: Just a Pinch Involved

Active Time: 45 minutes

Total Time: 45 minutes

Risotto is a rice dish made with a specific kind of Italian rice: Arborio. This recipe makes a thick, creamy risotto porridge that warms you up from the inside out.

INGREDIENTS

- 2 tablespoons unsalted butter
- 1 tablespoon extra virgin olive oil
- 3 small shallots, minced
- 3 ounces (6 slices) prosciutto, cut into bite-sized pieces
- 1 cup Arborio rice
- 4¼ cups **Chicken Stock** (p. 63), warm
- 2 cups fresh peas or frozen peas, thawed
- Handful mint, finely chopped
- Ground black pepper to taste (prosciutto is inherently salty so no extra salt is needed)
- Grated Parmesan cheese, as garnish

KIDS CAN

- Wash mint and spin dry
- Grate Parmesan with supervision
- Set the timer

WATCH OUT FOR

- Hot stove

INSTRUCTIONS

1. In a big pot, heat the butter and oil.
2. Add the shallot and prosciutto and sauté over medium heat until shallots are soft and slightly transparent, 3 to 5 minutes.
3. Add the rice, stirring continuously until rice is pan-fried and the rice grains are transparent.
4. Pour warm broth 1 cup at a time into the rice pot, stirring constantly until all the broth is absorbed.
5. Repeat this step until you have used 4 cups of the broth, the rice is smooth and the risotto itself is thick and shiny. This takes 20 minutes.
6. Stir in the peas, add the last ¼ cup of stock and cook uncovered until the rice and peas are tender, about 7 more minutes.
7. Reduce heat and let the risotto rest for a few minutes until all liquids have absorbed.
8. Ladle soup into bowls and serve with mint and grated Parmesan cheese as garnish.

NUTRITION NIBBLE Avocado and buttermilk give this vegetarian soup a decadent, buttery texture. These healthy fats are paired with fiber rich peas and spinach to make a surprisingly filling meal. Keep your kitchen stocked with frozen peas and vegetable broth to help you blend this soup together and get it on the table in no time.

PEA AND AVOCADO GAZPACHO

Makes: 3 cups
Contains: Milk
Diet Type: Gluten Free

Challenge Level: Piece of Cake
Active Time: 30 minutes
Total Time: 30 minutes

INGREDIENTS

- ½ cup fresh baby peas or frozen baby peas, thawed
- 1 English cucumber
- 4 handfuls (1 cup) baby spinach leaves
- 2 green onions
- 2 ripe avocados, divided
- ⅓ cup buttermilk
- 1 cup **Vegetable Broth** (p. 65)
- Juice of 1 lemon
- 1 small garlic clove, crushed
- Cracked black pepper to taste
- Cilantro, mint or parsley for garnish

KIDS CAN

- Wash greens and spin dry
- Grab handfuls of spinach
- Squeeze lemon
- Push button of the food processor with supervision

WATCH OUT FOR

- Sharp blades of the food processor or blender

INSTRUCTIONS

1. Blanch peas. Drop peas into a pot of boiling water. Cook 1 to 2 minutes. Immediately drain peas into a colander and rinse in cold water. Set aside.
2. Slice green onion (white and green parts) and cucumber.
3. Cut avocados in half. Carefully remove the seed and outer peel. Thinly slice the avocado.
4. Set one avocado aside to garnish the soup.
5. Put all of the other ingredients in a food processor or blender and pulse until smooth.
6. Garnish with fresh herbs and slices of avocado. Serve cold.

There was an Old Woman who lived in a Shoe

THERE WAS AN OLD WOMAN WHO LIVED IN A SHOE

There was an old woman who lived in a shoe.
She had so many children, she didn't know what to do;
She gave them some broth without any bread;
Then kissed them all soundly and put them to bed.

NUTRITION
NIBBLE

In essence, porotos con pilco is a thick vegetable soup made from frozen vegetables and legumes that comes together quickly for those days when you need a little extra love but don't have any extra time. From a nutrition standpoint, it contains just about everything you need in one bowl.

POROTOS CON PILCO

Makes: 8 cups

Contains: None of the Common Allergens

Diet Type: Gluten Free, Dairy Free

Challenge Level: Piece of Cake

Active Time: 15 minutes

Total Time: 1 hour

This soup is the ultimate comfort food. On those winter days when the temperature drops and it's dark by 5pm, I get out the soup pot and create this traditional, flavorful and filling Chilean soup. It's soothing, restorative and a meal in one bowl. This soup feels like a hug.

INGREDIENTS

- 1 tablespoon extra virgin olive oil
- 1 purple onion
- 1 garlic clove
- 3 cups frozen pumpkin (or butternut squash), cubed
- 3 cups frozen or fresh porotos granados
- 1 tablespoon dried oregano
- ½ tablespoon paprika
- 5 cups **Vegetable Broth** (p. 65) or water plus one low-sodium vegetable bouillon
- 1½ cups frozen green beans
- 1½ cups frozen corn
- Handful of fresh basil leaves, chiffonade

KIDS CAN

- Open frozen vegetables with kid-safe scissors
- Stir the soup
- Set the timer

WATCH OUT FOR

- Hot pot

INSTRUCTIONS

1. Finely chop the onion and garlic and sauté in a deep soup pot coated with extra virgin olive oil until soft, about 7 minutes.

2. Add dried oregano and paprika. Add frozen poroto granado beans, frozen pumpkin and vegetable broth.

3. Cover and simmer on medium heat for 15 minutes.

4. Add frozen green beans and corn. Cover the pot and continue to simmer for another 12 minutes.

5. Top with chopped basil and serve.

MOTHER GOOSE MIX UP

Porotos granados, also called pink beans or borlotti beans, have a beautiful hot pink pod with beans that are cream colored and streaked with red, magenta or black. If you can't find porotos granados where you live, use pinto beans as a substitute.

CHAPTER 4

Pasta AND Grains

You may have heard dietitians like me talking about simple versus complex carbohydrates. But what's the difference anyway? We digest and absorb simple carbohydrates (or "simple carbs") quickly, and turn them into energy for our bodies. A good example of a simple carb is table sugar, fruit juice or white bread. These carbs are great to eat when we need energy fast—like during soccer practice or before a swim meet. Complex carbs also come from fruits, vegetables, grains and cereals, but contain more fiber and starch. Complex carbs take longer to digest, so they keep our energy levels steady over more extended periods of time, which is important for learning and growing!

The recipes in this chapter make preparing food from complex carbs like couscous, whole grain rice and quinoa, simple. I've amped up the nutritional benefits of tried-and-true kid favorites like spaghetti and meatballs, pasta Alfredo and lasagna for sure-fire hits at the family table. I've also played on kids' natural affinity for pasta, grains, fruits and vegetables by creating a collection of salads that include these complex carbs in one-dish meals.

Remember, children need carbs, especially the good ones, from whole grains, cereals, fruit and vegetables. So, don't skimp on the fiber-filled, nutrient-rich and energizing recipes in this chapter!

ON TOP OF SPAGHETTI

ON TOP OF SPAGHETTI

On top of spaghetti,
All covered with cheese,
I lost my poor meatball
When somebody sneezed.

It rolled off the table
And onto the floor,
And then my poor meatball
Rolled right out the door.

It rolled through the garden
And under a bush.
Then my poor meatball
Turned into mush.

NUTRITION NIBBLE These meatballs wouldn't be the same without the carrot, onion and garlic—three vegetables which boost the flavor and nutritional value of this meaty pasta dish.

RUNAWAY MEATBALLS

Makes: 24 meatballs

Contains: Egg, Wheat

Diet Type: Dairy Free

Challenge Level: Piece of Cake

Active Time: 30 minutes

Total Time: 45 minutes

Let's face it, kids love to eat pasta! And meatballs are one of the most versatile ways to incorporate ground beef into a kid-friendly dinner. Consider this recipe your jumping off point for make-ahead meals for years to come. The key to meatballs is the meat to flour ratio. One pound of ground beef to 3 tablespoons flour is enough to keep your meatballs together, so they don't "turn into mush" and their texture stays soft but firm.

INGREDIENTS

- 1 pound ground beef, 85% lean
- 1 egg
- 3 tablespoons all-purpose flour
- ½ onion
- 2 garlic cloves
- 1 medium carrot
- 2 cups **Rich Red Sauce** (p. 211) or your favorite spaghetti sauce

KIDS CAN

- Mash the garlic with the back of a spoon
- Finely grate carrot with help
- Crack the egg
- Roll the balls (be sure to wash hands afterwards with soap and water)

WATCH OUT FOR

- Hot stove
- Wash hands with soap and water after handling raw meat
- Sharp blades of the grater

INSTRUCTIONS

1. Mince the onion. Mash the garlic. Grate the carrot.
2. Combine meat, grated carrot, garlic and onion in a large bowl.
3. Add the egg and flour. Sprinkle with salt and pepper to taste.
4. Mix together with your clean hands or a large spoon until all ingredients are incorporated.
5. Wet your hands in cold water. As long as your hands are wet (but not dripping) the meat won't stick to you.
6. Place a heaping tablespoon of meatball mixture in the palm of your hand. Roll the meat into balls.
7. Put a small amount of sauce into a saucepan, add meatballs, then top with more sauce.
8. Simmer meatballs in a covered saucepan until meatballs are no longer pink inside, about 20 minutes. Serve over a plate of pasta, **Zoodles** (p. 97) or cooked spaghetti squash.

TIP: TACKLE TOMATO STAINS BY SOAKING SPOT IN COLD WATER,
THEN USE A GREASE-CUTTING PRETREATER. WE LIKE SHOUT
ADVANCED GREASE BUSTING FOAM. WASH IN WARM WATER
WITH FABRIC-SAFE BLEACH.

NUTRITION
NIBBLE   Red sauce is a great place to add in extra veggies.
Especially leftover grilled or roasted ones—they add depth and flavor to the sauce.

RICH RED SAUCE

Makes: 5 cups

Contains: None of the Common Allergens

Diet Type: Gluten Free, Dairy Free

Challenge Level: Piece of Cake

Active Time: 1 hour

Total Time: 1 hour 15 minutes

INGREDIENTS

- 4 cups, about 4 large heirloom tomatoes, or (2) 14.5 ounce cans whole peeled tomatoes in juice
- 1 tablespoon extra virgin olive oil
- 1 onion, chopped
- 3 garlic cloves
- 2 tablespoons sundried tomato purée
- 1 tablespoon balsamic vinegar
- Splash of red wine (optional)
- Generous shake (½ teaspoon) dried oregano
- Generous shake (½ teaspoon) dried basil
- Salt and pepper to taste

KIDS CAN

- Search the kitchen for sauce ingredients
- Smash the charred tomatoes once they are cool
- Shake the herbs
- Push button on the food processor with supervision

WATCH OUT FOR

- Hot stove, hot tomatoes
- Sharp blades of the food processor
- Tomato sauce stains

INSTRUCTIONS

1. In a skillet or deep pan, add chopped onion and olive oil. Cook on low heat to start the caramelization process. Stir occasionally. Onions are ready when they are sweet and brown, about 30 minutes.

2. Char tomatoes on the grill (or roast in oven on high heat until skins have browned on one side). Once cool, smash tomatoes with the back of a spoon.

3. Add sundried tomato purée to the onions in the skillet. Stir and continue to cook on low heat for another 5 minutes.

4. Add wine, balsamic vinegar, garlic and charred or canned tomatoes with their juices to the onions. Shake in the dried herbs.

5. Cook on low heat for another 30 minutes or until flavors come together. Allow to cool.

6. Transfer contents of the skillet to a food processor. Pulse until desired smoothness is reached. *(**Tip:** Depending on the size of your food processor you may have to do this step in batches).*

7. Serve with **Runaway Meatballs** (p. 209). Store remaining tomato sauce in a lidded, glass jar and freeze for future use in recipes such as **Ratatouille Lasagna** (p. 219).

Will you walk into my parlor?

Will you walk into my parlor?

"Will you walk into my parlor?"

Said the spider to the fly.

"'Tis the prettiest parlor that ever you did spy.

The way into my parlor

Is up a winding stair;

And I have many curious things

To show you when you're there."

"Oh, no, no," said the little fly, "to ask me is in vain;

For who goes up your winding stair

Can ne'er come down again."

This rhyme is one of my personal favorites. I love the imagery of the spider web as a winding stair and the witty banter as the spider flatters the fly. When I went to create a recipe, I wanted to keep the imagery of the threads of a spider web and the blackness of the bugs, so I chose black and white spaghetti noodles in a creamy white sauce. Professional chef and friend Lorena Salinas, developed the kid-friendly but sophisticated Alfredo sauce.

BE MINDFUL OF THE CREAM THAT YOU USE FOR THIS RECIPE. YOU NEED IT TO BE 30-34% FAT SO THE SAUCE DOESN'T SPLIT.

NUTRITION NIBBLE

Kids love food that is colorful and tasty. So for this dish, I swap out half of the wheat pasta with a high-protein, gluten-free black bean spaghetti-shaped pasta. Mixing traditional spaghetti with one made from black beans makes the dish visually appealing and staves off picky eating. Small changes such as varying the shape or color of pasta help children gain confidence trying new things (it's a familiar food - pasta - served in an unfamiliar way).

BLACK AND WHITE PASTA ALFREDO

Makes: 4 cups
Contains:: Milk, Wheat

Challenge Level: Just a Pinch Involved
Active Time: 45 minutes
Total Time: 45 minutes

INGREDIENTS

- ½ cup whole milk
- ¾ cup cream
- 1 garlic clove
- 1 bay leaf
- Pinch freshly grated nutmeg
- 2 cloves
- Pepper to taste
- 5 tablespoons unsalted butter
- 1½ cups freshly grated Grana Padano or Parmigiano Reggiano
- 8 ounces dry or fresh pasta (we use a combination of black bean and traditional spaghetti noodles)
- Fresh thyme
- Pink and black peppercorns for garnish

KIDS CAN

- Grate the cheese with help
- Count cloves and bay leaf

WATCH OUT FOR

- Boiling water
- Sharp blades of the cheese grater

INSTRUCTIONS

1. Peel the garlic clove. With the side of a chef's knife, smash the garlic clove to open it up.
2. In a medium saucepan add milk and cream.
3. Add the garlic, bay leaf, nutmeg and cloves. Bring the pot to a light simmer for 10 minutes to infuse the milk and cream with the flavor of the garlic and spices.
4. Remove cloves and bay leaf. (**Tip:** *I pick them out with my fingers. You can also pass the sauce through a fine mesh strainer.*)
5. Melt the butter in a nonstick frying pan or wok and pull out a big, deep pot to cook the pasta.
6. Cook pasta in boiling, salted water.
7. Add the infused milk and cream to the frying pan and bring it to a simmer over medium heat.
8. After 2 minutes, add finely grated Parmesan cheese. The cheese will melt as you mix it in.
9. Taste, and shake in ground black pepper.
10. Check on the pasta. Carefully scoop one spaghetti out of the boiling pasta pot, run it under cool water and taste. If it is done (al dente), strain the rest.
11. Add cooked pasta to the pan of Alfredo sauce. Toss and stir to coat.
12. Serve pasta Alfredo with fresh thyme leaves, freshly ground black and pink peppercorns and, in our opinion, it's never too much to add extra grated Parmesan on top.

PIED PIPER

PIED PIPER

Pied Piper of Hamelin by Peter Combe

Now listen I'll tell you a tale
A story from a long time ago
In Hamelin there was a plague
A plague of dirty rats.

They ate all the cheese from the vats
And spoiled the ladies' chats
By speaking and shrieking and squeaking
In fifty different sharps and flats.

(Chorus)
Hundreds and hundreds and hundreds of rats
Cheeky and sneaky and ravenous rats
Fought with the dogs and they killed the cats
Hundreds and hundreds and hundreds of rats.

Then one day a stranger appeared
Dressed in bright yellow and red
Said he "The Pied Piper am I
And I can get rid of those rats".

~ Chorus ~

The piper stepped out in the street
Put his pipe to his lips and he played
He danced all the way across town...

The people of Hamelin cheered
And rang all the bells in the town
"Go" said the Mayor "and get poles
Poke out the nests and block up the holes".

So the piper went back to the Mayor
Who'd faithfully promised to pay
One thousand guilders reward
The Mayor said "Fifty is all you will get."

~ Chorus ~

The piper stepped out in the street
And once again started to play
And all over Hamelin town
Came the patter of tiny feet.

They followed the piper up Koppelberg Hill
A door in the mountain swung open until
All of the children were safely inside
Then that door in the mountain swung shut.

And that's how this sad story ends
Not one of those children returned
The lesson is clear to us all
A promise made is a promise kept.

Go to Peter's website to listen to him sing this rhyme!
http://www.petercombe.com.au/song/pied-piper-hamelin

NUTRITION NIBBLE Veggies in the sauce plus veggies in the filling equals veggies in your bellies—always a good thing. Plus ricotta is rich in omega-3, selenium (an antioxidant) and, of course, calcium to promote healthy bones!

RATATOUILLE LASAGNA

Makes: 12 slices
Contains: Milk, Egg, Wheat

Challengé Level: Just a Pinch Involved
Active Time: 1 hour
Total Time: 1 hour 45 minutes

INGREDIENTS

- 14 lasagna noodles
  (12 for the lasagna dish plus 2 extra for filling holes)
- Extra virgin olive oil for painting

For the Ratatouille Sauce:
- 2 tablespoons extra virgin olive oil
- 1 medium onion, diced
- 4 large garlic cloves, minced
- 1 medium zucchini, cubed
- 1 medium yellow squash, cubed
- 1 medium purple eggplant, cubed
- 1 jar (12 oz) roasted red peppers, drained and cubed (optional)
- 1 cup **Rich Red Sauce** (p. 211) or store-bought marinara sauce
- Handful of fresh basil leaves, chopped or torn

For the Cheese Filling:
- 2 cups low-fat ricotta cheese
- 2 eggs
- 1 cup grated Parmesan cheese
- ½ teaspoon dried oregano
- 2 cups shredded mozzarella cheese
- Salt and pepper to taste

KIDS CAN

- Wash vegetables and pat dry
- Crack eggs with help
- Help assemble the lasagna by layering noodles, scooping and spreading the sauce and cheese

WATCH OUT FOR

- Hot surfaces —let the baking dish cool before placing it on the table

INSTRUCTIONS ON NEXT PAGE

MOTHER GOOSE COOKING TIP

Making two lasagnas isn't much more work than making one! Double the recipe and make one lasagna to eat now and freeze the other to eat later. When "later" comes, preheat your oven to 400°F. Take the lasagna directly from the freezer and bake it covered with aluminum foil on the middle rack of your oven. Bake until the filling begins to sizzle and internal temperature reaches 165°F. At this point, remove the aluminum foil and bake for about 5 more minutes, until the top is well browned.

RATATOUILLE LASAGNA

INSTRUCTIONS

For the Noodles:

1. Bring a large pot of water to a boil. Add a pinch of salt and the lasagna noodles to the boiling water. Cook about 8 minutes.
2. Place a colander in the sink and a baking sheet next to the sink. Drizzle baking sheet with a little olive oil and smear it around to cover the entire surface.
3. Don't dump all the noodles together into the colander or they will stick together. Remove lasagna noodles from the pot one at a time, strain to remove excess water and lay side by side flat on the oiled baking sheet. (*Tip: This is a good time for little ones to leave the kitchen*).
4. Paint the top of each noodle with olive oil.
5. Repeat until all noodles are side by side.

For the Ratatouille Sauce:

6. In a large, deep skillet heat olive oil.
7. When olive oil is shimmering, add onion and cook for 3 minutes.
8. Add garlic, zucchini, squash and eggplant. Cook, stirring occasionally, until the vegetables have softened, but still maintain some crunch, about 7 minutes.
9. Stir in roasted red peppers, basil leaves and **Rich Red Sauce** or store-bought marinara.
10. Allow vegetables to simmer together and thicken, about 10 minutes.
11. While sauce and vegetables are simmering, prepare the cheese filling.

For the Cheese Filling:

12. This is easy! Use a whisk to whip together the eggs, ricotta, oregano and two types of cheese. You can use a hand whisk or an electric mixer. The fluffier the better.

To Assemble Lasagna:

13. Preheat the oven to 350°F and paint a large 9 x 13-inch baking dish with a little bit of extra virgin olive oil.
14. Spread a thin layer of Ratatouille Sauce, just enough to barely cover the bottom.
15. On top of the sauce, arrange 4 noodles side by side, slightly overlapping each one.
16. Spread one third of the cheese filling on top of the noodles. Top with a layer, thicker this time, of Ratatouille Sauce.
17. Continue layering 4 noodles, cheese and sauce until you have used them up (three layers). The final layer will be cheese.
18. Loosely cover the dish with aluminum foil and bake for 25 minutes.
19. Uncover and bake 15 minutes more. (*Tip: To get a golden-brown, cheesy layer on top, switch the oven to broil and cook about 5 extra minutes.*)
20. Allow the lasagna to cool for 15 minutes before slicing and serving. If any lasagna is left over, cover with aluminum foil and store in the refrigerator. Reheat leftovers in the oven to an internal temperature of 165°F or microwave before serving.

GEORGIE PURGIE

GEORGIE PORGIE

Georgie Porgie, pudding and pie,
Kissed the girls and made them cry,
When the boys came out to play,
Georgie Porgie ran away.

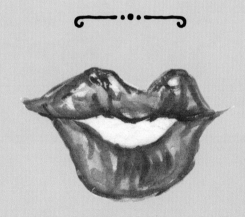

WHOLE GRAIN SALADS

Who said salads need to have lettuce? You can kiss that old fashioned notion goodbye! The base of these versatile dishes is whole grains and cereals, so they are hearty enough to stand alone if you'd like.

The coolest part? They're good for any meal, any time—brunch, lunch or dinner. Just whip out these recipes for a blast of plant-based nutrition.

NUTRITION
NIBBLE
I'm always looking for a way to incorporate fruit and vegetables into my recipes, not only for health reasons but also because, honestly, I'm a "lazy" cook, always looking for ways to pack it all into one dish. Why make a grain dish and a vegetable dish when I can combine them both into one bowl?

FIG AND QUINOA SALAD

Makes: 5 cups

Contains: Milk

Diet Type: Gluten Free

Challenge Level: Piece of Cake

Active Time: 20 minutes

Total Time: 45 minutes

INGREDIENTS

- 3 cups cooked **Basic Quinoa** (p. 87)
- 1 tablespoon extra virgin olive oil
- 8 figs, halved or quartered
- 8 strawberries, sliced or diced
- ½ cup sliced (or slivered) almonds
- 1 ripe avocado, peeled, pitted and sliced thin
- ½ block (6 ounces) feta, crumbled
- Freshly ground black pepper
- Juice of 1 lemon, more to taste

KIDS CAN

- Wash and dry produce
- Mix in fruit and almonds
- Crumble cheese

WATCH OUT FOR

- Sharp knives and hot stove

INSTRUCTIONS

1. Combine cooked quinoa and olive oil together in a large bowl. Set aside to cool if necessary.
2. Wash produce and pat dry.
3. Cut fruit and mix it into the cooked quinoa (**Tip:** *Wait to add the avocado until right before serving. A liberal squeeze of lemon will help preserve it's pretty green color.*)
4. Crumble feta cheese on top.
5. Serve at room temperature or cold with more fresh lemon juice.
6. Not suitable for storing (because avocado turns brown).

AVOCADO TABBOULEH

Makes: 3 cups

Contains: Wheat, Tree Nuts

Diet Type: Dairy Free

Challenge Level: Piece of Cake

Active Time: 30 minutes

Total Time: 1 hour

INGREDIENTS

- ⅔ cup chopped Persian or English cucumber
- ⅔ cup tomato, chopped
- ½ cup cooked **Basic Bulgur** (p. 90)
- ⅓ cup chopped parsley
- ¼ cup chopped mint
- 2 tablespoons finely chopped shallot
- Juice of ½ a lemon
- 2 tablespoons extra virgin olive oil
- Pinch of salt
- ½ ripe avocado, diced
- ⅓ cup chopped walnuts

KIDS CAN

- Wash and dry produce
- Separate parsley leaves from stems
- Peel the cucumber with help
- Squeeze the lemon
- Crush and sprinkle walnuts

WATCH OUT FOR

- No one telling you there are little green leaves stuck in your teeth

INSTRUCTIONS

1. Combine cucumber, tomato, Basic Bulgur, parsley, mint and shallot in a medium bowl.
2. Drizzle with lemon juice and oil. Sprinkle with salt.
3. Use clean hands or large spoons to combine.
4. Carefully tuck in avocado. (**Tip:** To keep the remaining half of the avocado green, squeeze a bit of lemon juice on it and cover, pit in place, with plastic wrap.)
5. Sprinkle with chopped walnuts.
6. Serve at room temperature.

GRILLED PEACH COUSCOUS

Makes: 6 cups

Contains: Wheat, Milk

Challenge Level: Piece of Cake

Active Time: 30 minutes

Total Time: 1 hour

INGREDIENTS

- 1 pound peaches, sliced (**Tip:** *firm peaches work best*)
- 3 cups beefsteak tomatoes (ideally a mix of colors), chopped
- 1½ cups cooked **Classic Couscous** (p. 89)
- ¼ bunch fresh basil
- 1 bunch fresh mint
- Salt and black pepper to taste
- ½ cup extra virgin olive oil
- ⅓ cup balsamic vinegar
- 1 cup crumbled **Paneer** (p. 239)

KIDS CAN

- Wash and dry produce
- Separate herb leaves from stems
- Crumble paneer

WATCH OUT FOR

- Hot grill

INSTRUCTIONS

1. Preheat grill to high 450°F and spray with cooking spray.
2. Cut peaches into thick wedges (you don't want peach pieces to fall through the grates).
3. Place peach slices on the oiled grill grates. Grill uncovered until grill marks appear, about 2 minutes per side. Set aside to cool.
4. In a large bowl combine chopped tomatoes, herbs and couscous.
5. When peaches are room temperature, cut into smaller pieces and add to the bowl with the tomatoes, couscous and herbs.
6. In a small, separate bowl, whisk together oil, vinegar, salt and pepper. Drizzle over the salad and gently toss to coat.
7. Top with crumbled paneer.

MOTHER GOOSE MIX UP

Add pomegranate seeds for a crunchy twist.

SOUTHWEST RICE SALAD

Makes: 3 cups
Contains: Milk, Egg
Diet Type: Gluten Free

Challenge Level: Piece of Cake
Active Time: 20 minutes
Total Time: 30 minutes

INGREDIENTS

For the Salad:
- ½ head broccoli
- 2 ears sweet corn
- ½ cup kale
- 1 cup cooked **Whole Grain (Brown) Rice** (p. 88)
- 1 tablespoon extra virgin olive oil, divided
- Salt and pepper
- ½ cup pumpkin seeds, toasted (**Tip:** *Sometimes pumpkin seeds are labeled as pepitas*)
- 1 cup canned black beans, drained and rinsed

For the Southwest Dressing:
- 2 tablespoons mayonnaise
- 1 tablespoon Greek yogurt or sour cream
- 2 teaspoons honey
- 1 teaspoon filtered water (or more to thin)
- ½ teaspoon apple cider vinegar
- ¼ teaspoon lime juice
- ¼ teaspoon onion powder
- ¼ teaspoon garlic powder
- ¼ teaspoon cayenne pepper
- ½ teaspoon cumin
- Extra lime for garnish

KIDS CAN
- Wash produce and pat dry
- Shuck the corn
- Pour dressing onto the salad and stir

WATCH OUT FOR
- Hot oven door and pans
- Sharp blades of blender

INSTRUCTIONS

1. Preheat oven to 450°F.
2. Shuck the corn, discard silks and stalks. Cut the kernels from the cob.
3. Rinse the broccoli. Pat dry. Trim broccoli stem and separate into florets. Pulse florets in batches in a food processor until broccoli resembles rice (you should have about 2 cups).
4. Put kale in food processor and pulse until finely chopped. Set aside.
5. Spread broccoli and corn on a large baking sheet. Sprinkle with salt, pepper and olive oil, then place in oven to roast.
6. Set timer for 8 minutes. While veggies roast, make the **Southwest Dressing**.
7. For the dressing, stir all the dressing ingredients together until incorporated.
8. Combine rice, veggies, black beans and toasted pumpkin seeds in a large bowl.
9. Pour dressing on top and stir to coat. Serve with slices of fresh lime.

CHAPTER 5

Tasty Veggies

It's an age-old problem: kids don't eat enough veggies and parents don't know what to do about it. These recipes are here to help! This is probably the chapter I am most proud of because, through the process of developing dishes and serving them to my family, my kids have learned to love veggies. They eat all of the foods on the following pages. These tasty veggie recipes give kids the ability to get involved in meal prep from scrubbing potatoes to picking herb leaves—so they develop a positive relationship with the greens (and reds, yellows, oranges and purples) on their plates.

Don't hide the veggies—celebrate them!

Here's a strategy that works well in our house. When Axel and Rex come to the table hungry, I set the vegetables out first. While I "finish up" the rest of the meal, they help themselves to broccoli, mushrooms, coleslaw, carrots or cucumber salad. Before I know it, I've got two little boys who have eaten all their veggies.

FIVE LITTLE DUCKS

FIVE LITTLE DUCKS

Five little ducks
Went swimming one day
Over the hills and far away
Mother duck said
"Quack, quack, quack, quack"
But only four little ducks
came swimming back.

Four little ducks
Went swimming one day
Over the hills and far away
Mother duck said
"Quack, quack, quack, quack."
But only three little ducks
came swimming back.

Three little ducks
Went swimming one day
Over the hills and far away
Mother duck said
"Quack, quack, quack, quack."
But only two little ducks
came swimming back.

Two little ducks
Went swimming one day
Over the hills and far away
Mother duck said
"Quack, quack, quack, quack."
But only one little duck
came swimming back.

One little duck
Went swimming one day
Over the hills and far away
Mother duck said
"Quack, quack, quack, quack."
But no little ducks
came swimming back.

Sad mother duck
Went swimming one day
Over the hills and far away
The sad mother duck said
"Quack, quack, quack, quack."
And ALL five little ducks
came swimming back.

1,2,3,4,5 INGREDIENT MEATLESS MEALS

These are counting recipes: each one has one more ingredient than the last.
As you count down in the rhyme, count up in the recipes! Disclaimer: salt, pepper
and extra virgin olive oil don't "count" as ingredients because, the way I see it,
there's not much worth eating that can be made without them!

NUTRITION NIBBLE Portobellos are one of the few dietary sources of vitamin D. Their nutrient profile supports a balanced immune system, which is so important for little kids. A quick note on the gills you find underneath the mushroom cap: some people scrape them off (use the back of a spoon), we eat them. Preferences are personal.

PORTOBELLO MUSHROOM STEAK

Makes: 2 servings

Contains: None of the Common Allergens

Diet Type: Gluten Free, Dairy Free

Challenge Level: Piece of Cake

Active Time: 15 minutes

Total Time: 15 minutes

The portobello mushroom is a steak among fungus! You'll find that the firm texture of portobello makes a delicious meat substitute, making it a cinch to incorporate more plant-based meals into your family's diet.

INGREDIENTS

- 2 large or 6 ounces portobello mushroom caps (1 for each person)
- 1 tablespoon extra virgin olive oil
- Pinch of salt and pepper

KIDS CAN

- Clean mushrooms
- Set timer

WATCH OUT FOR

- Hot stove
- Oil sputtering and popping out of the pan

INSTRUCTIONS

1. Wipe portobello caps with a damp cloth to remove excess dirt.
2. Cut into thick slices.
3. Drizzle portobellos with olive oil. Sprinkle with salt and pepper.
4. Warm a skillet or grill pan on medium heat and sear the portobellos for 5 minutes, turning often.
5. Optional: Eat as is or top with fresh herbs, Worcestershire sauce or balsamic glaze.

NUTRITION NIBBLE Cheese contains protein, calcium, zinc and vitamins A and B12. Fresh cheeses, such as paneer, goat cheese, feta, ricotta and cottage cheese, are among the most healthful choices since they are less processed. Kids love cheese and dairy is a food group that we tend to under-consume as we get older. Make eating fresh cheese a habit now and your kids will have stronger bones later.

PANEER

Makes: 12 ounces

Contains: Milk

Diet Type: Gluten Free

Challenge Level: Piece of Cake

Active Time: 30 minutes

Total Time: 45 minutes

Note: For this recipe you need a cheesecloth and a thermometer.

INGREDIENTS

- ½ gallon whole milk
- ¼ cup fresh lemon juice or white vinegar
- Pinch of salt

KIDS CAN

- Watch (from a safe distance) as the milk curds separate right before their very eyes—science in action!

WATCH OUT FOR

- Hot milk and steam

INSTRUCTIONS

1. Pour milk into a large saucepan and set over medium heat. Attach a thermometer to your pan or have one handy. Bring the milk to a gentle simmer, just below the boiling point of 212°F.

2. Stir milk occasionally, scraping the bottom of the pot to make sure it doesn't burn and stick to the bottom. When the milk is ready, it will make a dense foam and give off steam.

3. Remove milk from heat and stir in the lemon juice or vinegar. Stir once or twice. Watch the milk curdle!

4. Cover the saucepan and let milk stand for 10 minutes. If milk still has not separated completely, add more lemon juice or vinegar.

5. Strain curds through a cheesecloth over the sink or large mixing bowl. Gently rinse with cold water to help the paneer cool down.

6. Gather the loose ends of the cheesecloth in your hands and squeeze to remove excess liquid. Be careful, the paneer may still be hot!

7. Add salt, then transfer to a plate or dish and shape the curds into a rough circle. If you want a smooth paneer, set a second plate on top for 15 minutes, or up to an hour to press the curds flat.

8. Refrigerate and enjoy! Paneer can be eaten as cheese (see **Grilled Peach Couscous**, p. 229), can be cut into squares and used like tofu, or minced to use as a scrambled egg substitute.

NUTRITION NIBBLE   Aside from being quite low in calories, zucchini is an excellent source of vitamin C.

ZUCCHINI FINGERS

Makes: Makes 24 fingers
Contains: Egg, Wheat
Diet Type: Dairy Free

Challenge Level: Just a Pinch Involved
Active Time: 30 minutes
Total Time: 45 minutes

Chicken fingers appear on every kids' menu from Japanese restaurants to Italian; I am not making them at home too. Let's rethink the menu, shall we? Batons of fresh zucchini replace frozen, breaded chicken. Quickly pan-fry zucchini in whole grain breadcrumbs. You'll be amazed how these meatless "imposters" disappear just as fast their kids' menu counterparts.

INGREDIENTS

- 2 large zucchini
- 2 eggs
- 1 cup whole grain breadcrumbs
- Pinch of salt and pepper

KIDS CAN

- Wash zucchini and pat dry
- Crack eggs with help
- Pour breadcrumbs into one bowl

WATCH OUT FOR

- Another easy way to eat more vegetables!

INSTRUCTIONS

1. Cut zucchini lengthwise into batons, about ¼ inch thick and 3 inches long.
2. Set two shallow bowls side by side.
3. In first bowl, mix eggs, salt and pepper. Put breadcrumbs in the second bowl.
4. Spray a baking sheet with cooking spray.
5. Dip the zucchini in the egg bowl. Be sure to cover both sides, then dip into breadcrumbs.
6. Set the breaded zucchini on the baking sheet and repeat until all zucchini batons are breaded.
7. Heat a frying pan over medium heat with just enough olive oil to cover the bottom of the pan.
8. Pan fry zucchini batons in batches.
9. Serve "blow-on-it-hot" with a sprinkle of Parmesan cheese (optional) and a side of ketchup.

NUTRITION NIBBLE Low in carbs and packed with fiber and vitamins C and B6, cauliflower is a nutritional workhorse for the healthy cook.

CAULIFLOWER TACOS

Makes: 4 cups

Contains: None of the Common Allergens

Diet Type: Gluten Free, Dairy Free

Challenge Level: Piece of Cake

Active Time: 30 minutes

Total Time: 30 minutes

Riced, roasted or even raw, cauliflower shows off as a side dish and makes a great vegetarian main. It changed my life when my friend and cookbook collaborator Allie Rudney taught me to use it as a ground beef substitute. My family couldn't even tell the difference! To ease into meat substitutes, try replacing half the ground beef or turkey in your taco recipe with cauliflower.

INGREDIENTS

- 1 head (4 cups florets) of cauliflower
- 1 clove garlic, minced
- 1 onion, finely chopped
- Extra virgin olive oil, enough to coat the bottom of your pan
- 2 to 3 tablespoons taco seasoning
  (We like McCormick Gluten-Free Taco Seasoning)

KIDS CAN

- Wash cauliflower and pat dry
- Break cauliflower into florets
- Push the button on the food processor with supervision
- Choose taco toppings like shredded cheese, lettuce, tomatoes, avocados and sour cream

WATCH OUT FOR

- Sharp blades of the food processor

INSTRUCTIONS

1. Wash cauliflower and pat dry. Cut the head of cauliflower into pieces. Pulse in batches in a food processor until you have the consistency and size of ground meat.
2. Sauté onions and garlic in olive oil.
3. Add the cauliflower "meat" and cook for about 5 minutes so it is no longer crunchy but still firm.
4. Add taco seasoning and cook until flavors combine. Serve in tacos as a substitute for meat.

MOTHER GOOSE MIX UP Instead of taco seasoning mix, mix ground cauliflower "meat" into **Rich Red Sauce** (p. 211) for a vegetarian take on spaghetti bolognese!

NUTRITION NIBBLE Beets contain a bit of almost all the vitamins and minerals that you need and since they taste great, they are easy to incorporate into your diet. Beets can be roasted (like in this recipe), boiled, pickled, tossed in a salad or even enjoyed raw.

BEET BURGERS

Makes: 6 patties
Contains: Egg, Wheat
Diet Type: Dairy Free

Challenge Level: Just a Pinch Involved
Active Time: 30 minutes
Total Time: 30 minutes

INGREDIENTS

- 5 beets
- 1 can (14 ounces) black beans, drained and rinsed
- 2 cups panko
- 1 egg
- 2 tablespoons yellow mustard (or ketchup, BBQ sauce, etc.)
- Pinch of salt and pepper

KIDS CAN

- Scrub and wash beets
- Wrap beets in aluminum foil
- Smash black beans
- Set out condiments to dress the burgers (whole grain buns, spinach leaves, tomatoes, ketchup, mayonnaise, hot sauce, etc.)

WATCH OUT FOR

- Sharp blades of the food processor

INSTRUCTIONS

1. Wash beets and trim off the top and tail.
2. Loosely wrap beets in aluminum foil and bake at 350°F up to 1 hour. Beets are ready when you can easily pierce them with a fork.
3. Once cool, unwrap beets and discard the aluminum foil. Place beets in batches in a food processor (skins are edible) and pulse until you have a rough consistency.
4. In a separate bowl, smash the black beans with a fork.
5. Add in the egg, panko, mustard, salt and pepper and gently stir to combine.
6. Add the chopped beets and form into palm sized patties or make mini beet burgers. Set in fridge to firm up (5 minutes).
7. Heat skillet and drizzle with a little olive oil. Cook until firm and crisp on the outside, about 3 minutes per side.

SIMPLE SIMON

SIMPLE SIMON

Simple Simon met a pieman,
Going to the fair.
Said Simple Simon to the pieman,
"Let me taste your ware."

Said the pieman unto Simon,
"Show me first your penny."
Said Simple Simon to the pieman,
"Indeed I have not any."

Simple Simon went a-fishing,
For to catch a whale;
But all the water he had got
Was in his mother's pail.

Simple Simon went to look,
If plums grew on a thistle;
He pricked his fingers very much,
Which made poor Simon whistle.

He went for water in a sieve,
But soon it all fell through;
And now poor Simple Simon
Bids you all adieu.

NUTRITION NIBBLE What happens at the table... goes beyond the table! Making food together as a family and then sitting down to eat it, does more for your child than you might think. Research shows that children and adolescents who regularly eat meals with their parents tend to eat more fruits, vegetables and dairy products, and are less likely to be (or become) overweight. The benefits go beyond nutrition, too. Eating together can improve parent-child relationships by giving kids a sense of stability and connectedness.

BLACK BEAN AND ARTICHOKE ENCHILADA WREATH

Makes:	40 enchilada cones	**Challenge Level:**	So Worth the Effort
Contains:	Milk, Wheat	**Active Time:**	1 hour
		Total Time:	1 hour 30 minutes

If you're looking for finger-friendly, vegetarian party food you can make as a family, then look no further. The youngest child sprinkles the cheese, the older child adds a spoonful of filling, and a grown up or big kid rolls the tortillas into cones. A final family member smears on the enchilada sauce between the layers. Enchiladas bake while everyone cleans up for dinner.

INGREDIENTS

For the Enchilada Sauce:
- 3 tablespoons extra virgin olive oil
- 3 tablespoons toasted flour
  (or flour of your choice)
- 2 teaspoons ground chili powder
- 1 teaspoon cumin
- ½ teaspoon garlic powder
- ¼ teaspoon dried oregano
- ¼ teaspoon cayenne pepper
- ¼ teaspoon salt
- ¼ teaspoon ground cinnamon
- 2 tablespoons tomato paste
- 2 cups **Vegetable Broth** (p. 65)
- Freshly ground black pepper, to taste

For the Enchilada Wreath:
- ½ large onion, diced
- 3 garlic cloves, minced
- 6 artichoke hearts, cubed
- 2 bags fresh baby spinach
- 2 cups canned low-sodium black beans, drained and rinsed
- 1 aji verde (green chili pepper), seeds removed and minced
- 2 tablespoons sour cream (or natural yogurt)
- 20 tortillas
- 2 cups Mexican cheese blend or a mix of grated cheddar and a white cheese of your choice

KIDS CAN

- Wash and spin the spinach
- Drain and rinse the black beans
- Cut tortillas in half with kid-safe scissors and supervision
- Sprinkle cheese and spread sauce

WATCH OUT FOR

- Hot stove, hot oil and hot oven

INSTRUCTIONS ON NEXT PAGE

CREATE YOUR OWN DELICIOUS ENCHILADA SAUCE

KIDS CAN: CUT TORTILLAS TO MAKE THE CONES

INSTRUCTIONS

For the Enchilada Sauce:

1. In a small bowl, combine flour and spices.
2. Open the tomato paste and measure the vegetable broth. Place them near your stove.
3. Heat a medium saucepan and add olive oil. When oil begins to shimmer, test with a pinch of the flour and spice blend. If it sizzles, add the rest.
4. Whisk or stir constantly for about 30 seconds. Add in the tomato paste and whisk until incorporated.
5. Pour in the vegetable broth.
6. Make sure the sauce is simmering and does not boil.
7. Cook, whisking constantly, until mixture is thickened and passes the "Spoon Test" (see p. 35). Transfer to a small bowl and allow to cool. (**Tip:** *I know this sounds like a lot of whisking but the sauce comes together quickly, no more than 10 minutes.*)

For the Black Bean Filling:

8. In a deep-sided skillet, sauté the onion and garlic until fragrant, about 3 minutes.
9. Add the artichoke, aji verde and black beans.
10. Toss in the spinach one handful at a time. Once the spinach has cooked down, remove the skillet from heat.
11. Stir in sour cream and shake on salt and pepper. (**Tip:** *This isn't immediately flavorful as is, but with the sauce and cheese, yum!*)

BLACK BEAN AND ARTICHOKE ENCHILADA WREATH

INSTRUCTIONS

To Create the Wreath:

12. Preheat oven to 350°F. Cut tortillas in half with kid-safe scissors. Line a pizza pan with parchment paper. Place a medium sized oven-safe bowl upside down in the middle of the pan. (The bowl marks the center. Set the enchilada cones around it to create the wreath.)

13. Now assemble the enchilada cones.

14. Set half a tortilla on a clean surface and sprinkle it with cheese. Place a spoonful of enchilada filling in the center and smoosh it down with the back of the spoon. Roll the tortilla in the shape of a cone. Don't overfill. Place the cone, pointy side facing the center bowl, on the parchment paper. Continue to add cones, making a ring all the way around the bowl.

15. Spread some enchilada sauce on top of the first layer of cones (a silicon paint brush or the back of a wooden spoon will work well for this task).

16. Continue to layer enchilada cones on top of the first ring until you make a second layer around the central bowl. Paint enchilada sauce on top of the second layer and sprinkle with cheese.

17. Flip over the center bowl and fill it with the remaining enchilada sauce. This serves two purposes: the bowl will prevent any cones from sliding out of place, and it holds the extra sauce for dipping.

18. Place the wreath and extra sauce in the oven. Bake until the cheese melts, about 20 minutes.

19. Carefully grab the parchment paper under the enchilada wreath. Pull and slide the wreath from the hot pizza pan onto a serving dish (support the underside of the wreath with a spatula). Family and friends can serve themselves by pulling out individual cones.

MOTHER GOOSE MIX UP

To make meaty enchiladas, cook ground beef with taco seasoning, and diced onion. Fill the halved tortillas as usual with cheese, then add the meat and roll into cones. Don't forget the layer of enchilada sauce between each ring!

LADYBIRD

LADYBIRD

Ladybird, ladybird fly away home,
Your house is on fire and your children are gone.
All except one,
And her name is Ann,
And she hid under the frying pan!

This recipe is every supermom's answer to the end of the week pile of vegetables that are still sitting on the counter or left forgotten in the crisper drawer of the refrigerator. An overabundance of almost too-ripe vegetables often plagues my kitchen. And this recipe helps keep us from wasting any of the fresh-market veggies we buy. Stir Fry is a dish so versatile you can serve it as a main meal with brown rice (or rice noodles), or enjoy it as a side dish. I've included our ideal list of veggies, but feel free to use what you have lying around, and you'll never have to see good vegetables go bad again *(**Tip:** Stir Fry works best if you have at least two different vegetables plus one leafy green.)*

NUTRITION NIBBLE This dish is made of lots and lots of vegetables—'nuff said! Cook up a batch of **Whole Grain (Brown) Rice** (p. 88) to serve alongside this healthy and colorful dish.

VEGGIE STIR FRY

Makes: 10 cups

Contains: Wheat, Soy, Fish (fish sauce)

Diet Type: Dairy Free

Challenge Level: Piece of Cake

Active Time: 45 minutes

Total Time: 45 minutes

INGREDIENTS

For the Skillet:

- 2 tablespoons vegetable oil
- ½ yellow onion, diced
- 2 cloves garlic, minced
- 1 finger (2 inches) fresh ginger, minced or grated
- ½ cup **Vegetable Broth** (p. 65) or store-bought
- 2 carrots, peeled and cut into coins
- 1 red bell pepper, seeds removed, cut into strips
- ½ head broccoli, cut into florets
- ½ zucchini cut into bite-sized chunks
- 1 pack (about 8 ounces) mushrooms, sliced
- ½ large bunch of chard, rinsed, stems removed, and roughly cut with kid-safe scissors
- Sesame seeds, for garnish

For the Sauce:

This one's easy! Combine these ingredients in a lidded jar and shake until mixed.

- 2 tablespoons coconut or white vinegar
- ¼ cup low-sodium soy sauce
- 1 teaspoon fish sauce
- 1 tablespoon honey
- 1 teaspoon sesame oil
- 1 teaspoon mirin
- 2 cloves garlic, minced
- 1 finger (about 2 inches) piece of ginger, minced or grated

KIDS CAN

- Wash vegetables and pat or spin dry
- Cut chard with kid-safe scissors and supervision
- Shake the sauce

WATCH OUT FOR

- Hot skillet and sharp knives

INSTRUCTIONS ON NEXT PAGE

VEGGIE STIR FRY

CONTINUED

INSTRUCTIONS

1. Prep the veggies: Cut the onion, garlic and ginger and put together in a bowl. Wash the carrots, bell peppers, broccoli, mushrooms and zucchini and pat dry. Cut into shapes listed and combine in another bowl. In a salad spinner, wash and rinse the chard. Roughly chop the chard with kid-safe scissors and set aside. (**Tip:** *I give myself 20 minutes for this step.*)

2. Heat a skillet or wok over medium-high on the stove, about 2 minutes. Pour in enough vegetable oil to swirl around and coat the bottom.

3. Add onion, garlic and ginger, then sauté 3 minutes.

4. Lower heat to medium, add broth and dump in all the chopped vegetables, except the chard. Set timer for 8 minutes.

5. While vegetables cook, combine all sauce ingredients in a jar with a lid, put on your favorite dance song and shake, shake, shake!

6. Occasionally stir the vegetables in the skillet. **Note:** if veggies are sticking to the skillet, add some more broth, but don't let the Stir Fry get soggy.

7. When timer sounds, add the chard and half of the sauce. Reduce heat to low then reset timer and cook 8 minutes more or until chard shrinks and vegetables are tender, but firm. Turn off heat.

8. Sprinkle with sesame seeds and serve on its own, or with rice or noodles (vermicelli). Set extra sauce on the table. The leftovers for this recipe taste great cold or reheated in the microwave.

MOTHER GOOSE MIX UP

Try subbing the Stir Fry sauce for the sauce from
Spaghetti Squash Shrimp Pad Thai (p. 347). Yum!

PETER, PETER, PUMPKIN EATER

PETER, PETER, PUMPKIN EATER

Peter, Peter, pumpkin eater,
Had a wife and couldn't keep her.
He put her in a pumpkin shell,
And there he kept her very well.

Peter, Peter, pumpkin eater,
Had another and didn't love her.
Peter learned to read and spell,
And then he loved her very well.

NUTRITION NIBBLE In North America it's uncommon to eat pumpkin unless it's in a pie, but in Chile, pumpkin is incorporated into soups, salads and breads. In other words, it works perfectly in sweet and savory dishes or dishes that mix sweet and savory together like this one. High in fiber and rich in vitamins, minerals and antioxidants, pumpkin can help protect eyesight and promote heart and skin health.

HONEY-SPICED ROASTED PUMPKIN

Makes: 4 cups

Contains: Milk, Tree Nuts

Diet Type: Gluten Free

Challenge Level: Just a Pinch Involved

Active Time: 45 minutes

Total Time: 1 hour 30 minutes

INGREDIENTS

- 1 pound sugar pumpkin, sliced, skin on
- ½ cup dark brown sugar
- ½ cup walnuts, roughly chopped
- 1 tablespoon honey
- ½ teaspoon cinnamon
- ½ teaspoon nutmeg
- ½ teaspoon allspice
- ¼ teaspoon ground cloves
- 1 ball (8 ounces) buffalo mozzarella

KIDS CAN

- Wash pumpkin
- Scoop out seeds
- Sprinkle sugar and spice blend
- Tear and place mozzarella with the pumpkin before serving

WATCH OUT FOR

- Hot oven and sharp knives
- Slippery, raw pumpkin seeds can be a choking hazard. Make sure they stay out of little mouths.

INSTRUCTIONS

1. Preheat oven to 350°F. Rinse pumpkin under warm water to remove any dirt. Pat dry and cut in half.
2. Scoop out seeds from the center (save if you want to roast them later) and cut the pumpkin into wedge shaped slices following along the pumpkin's natural ridges. Set aside.
3. In a small bowl, combine brown sugar, cinnamon, nutmeg, allspice and cloves. Mix well.
4. Spread pumpkin wedges in a deep baking dish and use your sifter or fine-mesh colander to liberally sprinkle the sugar and spice mixture over each wedge.
5. Drizzle honey on top of everything.
6. Bake for 45 to 60 minutes or until the pumpkin wedges are caramelized and tender.
7. While pumpkin bakes, toast walnuts in a dry non-stick pan over medium heat. When walnuts are fragrant, remove them from heat, about 6 minutes.
8. Serve the pumpkin on a plate and spoon some of the sugar-spiced baking juices on top. Sprinkle with toasted walnuts, and decorate with chunks of torn buffalo mozzarella.

ONE POTATO, TWO POTATO

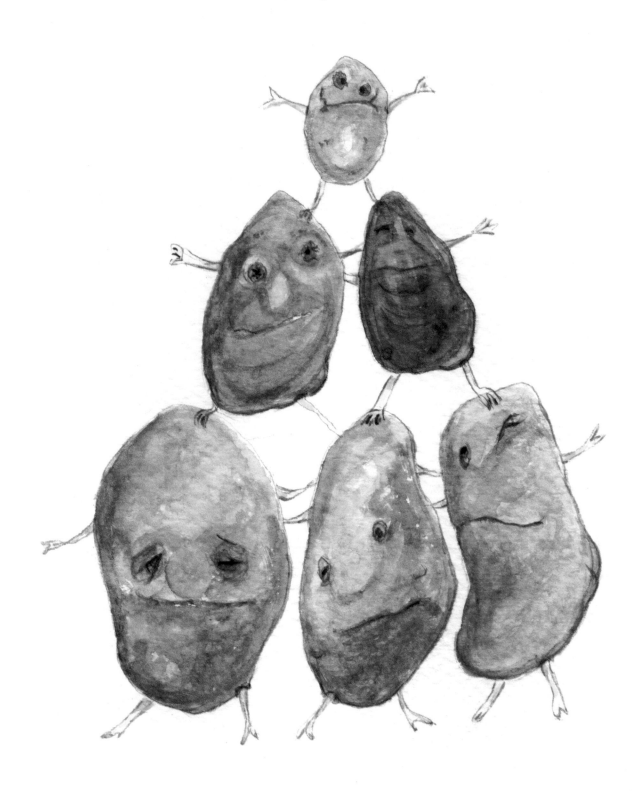

ONE POTATO, TWO POTATO

One potato, two potatoes,

three potatoes, four.

Five potatoes, six potatoes,

seven potatoes, more.

Potatoes are very popular with kids. These recipes serve up a
variety of potatoes in a rainbow of colors.

NUTRITION NIBBLE

One: Potatoes are a great source of
carbohydrates—a good thing that's getting
a bad rap lately. Carbs fuel both brains and
bodies and are the primary source of energy
for growth and sports.

Two: Potatoes have B Vitamins which help your
body put carbs to work to provide you energy
and keep you healthy.

Three: Potatoes are a source of Vitamin C—an
essential micronutrient for healthy skin, bones
and hair.

Four: Potatoes have lots of fiber.
Everybody needs it. You know why. (Wink)

Five: Potatoes contain folate which helps
your body make red blood cells.

Six: Potatoes are relatively inexpensive and,
with over 4,000 varieties to choose from,
you'll be sure to find some your family likes.

Seven: Potatoes have kid-appeal, and as a key
part of each of these yummy recipes, your kids
are sure to eat them.

SWEET POTATO FRIED RICE

Makes: About 3 cups

Contains: Milk, Egg, Soy

Diet Type: Gluten Free option

Challenge Level: Piece of Cake

Active Time: 20 minutes

Total Time: 30 minutes

INGREDIENTS

- 1 tablespoon dark sesame seed oil
- 1 tablespoon vegetable oil
- 2 large sweet potatoes
- 1 cup Swiss chard, about 3 large leaves
  (**Tip:** *If you can't find chard in your local market, swap in a mix of spinach and arugula.*)
- 1 medium carrot
- 2 green onions, green and white parts, sliced thin
- ⅛ cup chives, sliced thin
- 2 eggs
- 2 tablespoons soy sauce or certified gluten-free tamari sauce

KIDS CAN

- Scrub and dry the potato
- Count the Swiss chard leaves
- Wash and spin chard
- Use kid-safe scissors to cut chives with supervision

WATCH OUT FOR

- Sharp blades of the food processor

INSTRUCTIONS

1. Scrub dirt off sweet potatoes and pat dry.
2. Remove potato skins with a vegetable peeler then roughly chop them (**Tip:** *Prechop to be nice to the food processor*). Pulse until potatoes look like rice.
3. Peel the carrot, then grate it.
4. Remove 3 large chard leaves from the bunch. Cut out the ribs and discard. Roughly chop the chard leaves, then rinse and run through your salad spinner.
5. Rinse the chives and cut into tiny pieces using kid-safe scissors or a sharp knife.
6. Heat a non-stick frying pan or skillet over medium heat. Add sesame and vegatable oils.
7. Add half the green onions and all the sweet potato rice. Cook for 5 minutes.
8. Crack and whisk the eggs in a small bowl.
9. Add eggs, grated carrot and the rest of the onions to the frying pan. Cook for 5 more minutes.
10. Stir the "rice" and add a handful of chard every couple of minutes until you've added it all.
11. Pour in soy sauce, stir to incorporate and remove from heat.
12. Sprinkle with chives before serving.

ROASTED BRUSSELS SPROUTS AND POTATOES

Makes: 4 cups

Contains: None of the Common Allergens

Diet Type: Gluten Free, Dairy Free

Challenge Level: Piece of Cake

Active Time: 35 minutes

Total Time: 1 hour

INGREDIENTS

- 2 cups Brussels sprouts, halved
- 2 cups baby potatoes, chopped

For the Dressing:
- 2 tablespoons balsamic vinegar
- 2 tablespoons grainy mustard
- 2 tablespoons extra virgin olive oil
- 2 tablespoons maple syrup
- ½ tablespoon fresh rosemary
- ½ tablespoon fresh thyme
- 1 teaspoon black pepper
- ¼ teaspoon sea salt

KIDS CAN

- Wash and dry potatoes and Brussels sprouts
- Remove outer leaves from sprouts
- Set the timer

WATCH OUT FOR

- Hot oven
- Sharp knives

INSTRUCTIONS

1. Wash sprouts and potatoes. Chop the top and tail off the Brussels sprouts and remove outer leaves. Cut Brussels sprouts in half and rinse again. Set aside to dry.

2. Chop potatoes to the same size as Brussels sprout halves.

3. Preheat oven to 375°F and line two baking sheets with parchment paper or silpat.

4. Spread the Brussels sprouts on one sheet and the potatoes on the other.

5. Whisk together dressing ingredients. Pour half over the Brussels sprouts and half over the potatoes. Mix them up to coat evenly (**Tip:** *if your family loves sauce, make extra for the table*).

6. Place the potatoes in the oven. Set a timer for 10 minutes. When timer sounds, rotate the potato pan and add the pan with the Brussels sprouts.

7. Set a new timer for 20 minutes. Check tenderness by stabbing potatoes and Brussels sprouts with a fork. If the fork inserts easily, they are ready. If not, continue to roast for 5 to 10 minutes more. Serve warm with extra sauce (optional).

POTATO SOUP

Makes: 4 cups
Contains: Milk
Diet Type: Gluten Free

Challenge Level: Piece of Cake
Active Time: 20 minutes
Total Time: 30 minutes

INGREDIENTS

- 1 tablespoon extra virgin olive oil
- 1 medium onion, quartered
- 1 garlic clove, halved
- 1 medium potato, peeled and quartered
- 1 head lettuce, washed
  (use a mix of leafy greens or simply iceberg)
- ½ tablespoon dried tarragon
- 1 cup **Vegetable Broth** (p. 65) or store-bought
- 3 to 4 cups cold filtered water
- 1 container plain unsweetened Greek yogurt
- Chopped parsley leaves, to taste

KIDS CAN

- Scrub and dry the potato
- Wash and spin the lettuce
- Add the cold water

WATCH OUT FOR

- Sharp blades of the blender
- Transfering hot liquid soup into blender

INSTRUCTIONS

1. In a large, deep pot add olive oil, onion and garlic. Sauté for about 3 minutes.
2. Add broth, water, tarragon and potatoes. Bring to a boil, then lower to medium heat.
3. When a knife passes easily through the potatoes, add lettuce and cook another 1 minute so the leaves become soft.
4. Remove the pot from heat.
5. Pour the contents of the pot into a blender (in batches if you have to) and process until you get a smooth soup.
6. Before serving, place a few spoonfuls of Greek yogurt in the bottom of each soup bowl, sprinkle with parsley and then pour the soup on top. Serve warm.

TRUFFLE FRIES

Makes: 3 cups

Contains: Milk

Diet Type: Gluten Free

Challenge Level: Piece of Cake

Active Time: 30 minutes

Total Time: 30 minutes

INGREDIENTS

- 2 pounds small potatoes in a variety of colors
- 4 tablespoons extra virgin olive oil
- 1 teaspoon sea salt
- ½ teaspoon freshly ground pepper
- 2 tablespoons truffle oil or to taste
- ¼ cup fresh parsley, chopped
- ¼ cup Parmesan cheese, finely grated

KIDS CAN

- Scrub and dry potatoes
- Sprinkle Parmesan cheese and parsley

WATCH OUT FOR

- Hot oil can splatter

INSTRUCTIONS

1. Scrub potatoes and pat dry.
2. Cut the potatoes into wedges, careful to make each wedge the same size.
3. In a mixing bowl, toss the potatoes with olive oil, salt and pepper.
4. Heat a nonstick frying pan and add potatoes in batches, careful not to overcrowd. You may need to add a bit of oil to your pan between each batch.
5. Pan fry for 10 minutes or until potatoes have a golden glow, crispy outside and tender inside (**Tip:** *A fork should easily pierce the wedges*).
6. As soon as potatoes come out of the pan, drizzle with truffle oil and sprinkle with Parmesan cheese and parsley.
7. Use tongs to toss potatoes (so you don't burn your hands) to ensure each one gets the truffle-Parmesan flavor. Best served "blow-on-it-hot".

PETER PIPER

PETER PIPER

Peter Piper picked a peck of pickled peppers;
A peck of pickled peppers
Peter Piper picked.
If Peter Piper picked a peck of pickled peppers.
Where's the peck of pickled peppers Peter Piper picked?

I love to play around with bell peppers, which are native to Central and South America. Bell peppers are sweet, colorful (they come in yellow, orange, red, and green), and fun for kids because they are sweet and tasty even when raw. Offering a variety of colors when it comes to vegetables increases acceptance and nutritional value. This is my take on the Romesco of Catalonia, Spain, with ingredients I find in my local supermarket. The Spanish put Romesco over fish, but we love this salsa over Roasted Asparagus.

P.S.   A peck of peppers is about 2 gallons.

NUTRITION NIBBLE Romesco is made with fresh bell peppers and tomato, which are mainly composed of water—the rest is carbs and small amounts of protein and fat. When you combine bell peppers with hazelnuts, almonds and extra virgin olive oil you get a well-balanced salsa with health benefits for your heart, eyes and digestive system. The power of veggies is real, folks. Load up!

ROMESCO SALSA

Makes: 4 cups salsa
Contains: Tree Nuts
Diet Type: Gluten Free, Dairy Free

Challenge Level: Piece of Cake
Active Time: 30 minutes
Total Time: 30 minutes

INGREDIENTS

- 1 handful (¼ cup) toasted almonds
- 1 handful (¼ cup) toasted hazelnuts
- 3 red bell peppers
- 1½ pounds ripe Roma tomatoes
  (*Tip: Roma tomatoes have less juice so they're better for making sauces*)
- 1 handful chopped cilantro stems and leaves
- 2 cloves garlic
- ½ cup extra virgin olive oil
- 4 tablespoons red wine vinegar
- Salt and ground black pepper to taste

KIDS CAN

- Grab almonds and hazelnuts by the handful
- Choose the ripest tomatoes
- Count the bell peppers
- Wash cilantro and spin dry
- Push the button on the food processor with supervision

WATCH OUT FOR

- Sharp knives and processor blades
- Hot oven

INSTRUCTIONS

1. Preheat the oven to 450°F.
2. In a dry, non-stick frying pan, spread almonds and hazelnuts in an even layer and toast until golden and aromatic, about 10 minutes.
3. Transfer nuts to a bowl and set aside to cool.
4. Spread the uncut bell peppers and whole tomatoes on a baking sheet and roast until charred on one side and soft, 5 to 10 minutes.
5. Transfer the vegetables to a bowl and cover with a dry kitchen towel so they steam. When cool enough to touch, slip off the tomato and pepper skins and discard.
6. Cut open charred veggies and remove excess seeds.
7. Wash the cilantro and spin dry.
8. Combine all the ingredients in a food processor with the cilantro and pulse.
9. Add the vinegar, salt and pepper. Pulse until you get a coarse salsa with some chunks. (*Tip: The sweetness of tomatoes and bell peppers varies with the season. If you taste the romesco and the vinegar flavor is too strong, add a pinch of sugar*).
10. Serve over roasted asparagus (next page), on chicken and fish or with chips. Keep in mind, romesco is even better the next day.

ROASTED ASPARAGUS

Makes: 1 bunch, about 12 spears

Contains: None of the Common Allergens

Diet Type: Gluten Free, Dairy Free

Challenge Level: Piece of Cake

Active Time: 5 minutes

Total Time: 15 minutes

A quick note about asparagus: thin spears cook quickly, thick spears need more time. If you're not sure, stab a spear with a fork, careful not to burn yourself. Blow on it before you take a taste. When it tastes "right" to you, remove from the oven. Asparagus is best served "blow-on-it-hot".

INGREDIENTS

- 1 bunch of asparagus
- 1 teaspoon vegetable seasoning blend
  (We like McCormick Garden Vegetable Seasoning)
- Cooking spray or extra virgin olive oil

KIDS CAN

- Wash the asparagus spears
- Shake on their favorite vegetable seasoning

WATCH OUT FOR

- Hot oven and hot food

INSTRUCTIONS

1. Preheat oven to 375°F. Wash asparagus and trim the woody end opposite the tip.
2. Spray baking sheet with cooking spray.
3. Lay asparagus side by side on a baking sheet, allowing the spears to touch.
   Spray the asparagus with cooking spray or drizzle with olive oil.
4. Liberally shake on vegetable seasoning.
5. Place the baking sheet on the center rack of the oven and cook for 8 minutes for asparagus that is toasted, bright green and crunchy.

THE OWL AND THE PUSSYCAT

THE OWL ⟨AND⟩ THE PUSSYCAT

The Owl and the Pussycat went to sea
In a beautiful pea-green boat,
They took some honey, and plenty of money,
Wrapped up in a five-pound note.
The Owl looked up to the stars above,
And sang to a small guitar,
"O lovely Pussycat! O Pussycat, my love,
What a beautiful Pussycat you are,
You are,
You are!
What a beautiful Pussycat you are!"

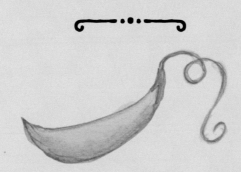

Sweet, soft, green peas—my boys love them, but didn't always. The journey from refusal to "more peas please" is a classic example of food exposure. First, they watched me shell peas outside while they dug in the dirt, playing "construction site". They helped by putting the empty pods in their toy dump trucks and driving them to the trash. When Axel and Rex were finally ready to try peas, I let them use their fingers. Peas are frustrating to scoop and stab. It takes a lot of patience to watch your child eat One. Pea. At. A. Time.

But, if patience wasn't easily tested, it wouldn't be a virtue, and I am proud to say that Honey Peas are now scooped in by the spoonful with an ardent "YAY!" and mouths wide open.

HONEY PEAS

Makes: About 2 cups
Contains: Tree Nuts
Diet Type: Gluten Free

Challenge Level: Piece of Cake
Active Time: 15 minutes (longer if shelling peas)
Total Time: 15 minutes

INGREDIENTS

- 2 cups fresh or frozen peas
- 1 tablespoon unsalted butter, melted
- 1 tablespoon honey
- Handful pecans, chopped or crushed with the back of a spoon
- Pinch each of ginger, nutmeg, and garlic powder
- Fresh mint for garnish

KIDS CAN

- Wash and shell peas
- Push the start button on microwave
- Separate mint leaves from stems
- Pinch the spices
- Taste spiced honey butter

WATCH OUT FOR

- Hot water and hot stove

INSTRUCTIONS

1. Wash and shell fresh peas or take out a bag of frozen peas.
2. In a medium saucepan, bring water to a boil. Pour in the peas. Set timer for 4 minutes.
3. Meanwhile, in a microwave-safe dish, heat butter with the spices until the butter starts to melt. Stir to continue the melting.
4. Dip a tablespoon in the melted butter to coat it, then pour honey on the buttered spoon (the butter coating will make all the honey slide off the spoon).
5. Stir the honey into the butter and spices. Taste. Add more of whatever you like.
6. When the timer goes off, turn off heat, spoon out a few peas, rinse under cold water, and taste. If the peas are too crunchy, put them back in the hot water for another minute.
7. If peas are perfect (not mushy) strain them using a colander.
8. Transfer peas to a skillet (or put back in the same saucepan), pour in the spiced honey butter, toss in the pecans, stir and serve warm with mint leaves as a garnish.

THREE BLIND MICE

Three Blind Mice

Three blind mice, three blind mice!
See how they run, see how they run!
They all ran after the farmer's wife,
Who cut off their tails with a carving knife.
Did you ever see such a sight in your life,
As three blind mice?

Farmer's Wife Chopped Salads

Here is a great opportunity to help your little one build dexterity and skills in the kitchen. So, make like the farmer's wife and use the carving knife. These recipes are ideal for your child to practice because the veggies aren't too slippery and can be cut using a kid-friendly knife. On page 46 you'll find photos of each of the cuts mentioned in the recipes so you can reference.

THE PERSIAN CUCUMBER IS A SMALL CUCUMBER WITH TENDER "NO PEEL" SKIN THAT IS VIRTUALLY SEEDLESS.

NUTRITION NIBBLE

Many kids learn to eat veggies plain with a dip on the side, but this salad is going to change all that. Help your child explore new flavors and textures in food by offering familiar foods (like cucumbers) in unfamiliar ways, like in a salad. Let your child get involved by chopping cucumbers with a sturdy plastic knife and he or she will be even more keen to take a taste.

Thai Cucumber Salad

Makes:	5 cups	**Challenge Level:**	Piece of Cake
Contains:	Wheat, Soy, Fish (fish sauce)	**Active Time:**	30 minutes
Diet Type:	Dairy Free	**Total Time:**	40 minutes

This cucumber salad is a staple in our house, and no one makes it better than my mother-in-law whose famous cucumber salad is world renowned. Some grandmas make cookies with their grandchildren, but our "Mimi" respects how important it is for her grandsons to eat their veggies. So, with lots of chopping, plucking, picking and mixing they get to work (and play) in the kitchen. Besides, we can always make cookies later.

INGREDIENTS

For the Salad:
- 1 medium purple onion, sliced
- 3 bags (about 4 cups) Persian cucumbers
- 2 handfuls fresh cilantro, minced
- 2 handfuls (½ cup) toasted pumpkin seeds
- 1 medium aji verde (green chili pepper) seeded and brunoise
- ½ teaspoon salt
- ½ teaspoon black pepper

For the Dressing:
- ¼ cup fresh lime juice, from 3 limes
- 2 tablespoons extra virgin olive oil
- ½ tablespoon fish sauce
- 1 to 2 tablespoons granulated sugar
- 1 garlic clove, minced

KIDS CAN

- Learn different knife cuts under adult supervision
- Soak the onions
- Wash and seed the cucumbers
- Grab the pumpkin seeds (in which case you might want 2 handfuls)
- Measure and whisk dressing ingredients

WATCH OUT FOR

- Even kid-friendly knives can be sharp. Guide your child's hands as he or she chops ingredients for this salad

INSTRUCTIONS ON NEXT PAGE

THAI CUCUMBER SALAD CONTINUED

INSTRUCTIONS

1. Top and tail the onion. Then cut the onion in half.

2. Pull off the papery skin on the outside of the onion and discard.

3. Set onion cut-side down so it lies flat against the cutting board. Carefully slice into the onion at a 45-degree angle, curling your fingers so your knuckles can guide the knife. (**Tip:** *this is best left to grown-ups.*)

4. Put the cut onion in a bowl of cold water. Set a timer for 10 minutes and let the onion soak. This mellows the onion's flavor.

5. Meanwhile, wash the cucumbers and pat them dry. Cut in half lengthwise.

6. Point a small spoon straight down over the exposed row of seeds and drag it along the row pushing down slightly. This will scrape the seeds out without breaking the cucumber.

7. Slice the seeded cucumber into crescent moons about ¼ inch thick.

8. Grab a big handful of cilantro and mince the leaves and stems together. (**Tip:** *there is a lot of flavor in the cilantro stems, so use them.*)

9. Brunoise cut the aji verde. If you like more spice, include the seeds, if not, toss them in the garbage and wash your hands after.

10. In a small bowl, combine all dressing ingredients and whisk until sugar is dissolved. Drain the onions and combine all salad ingredients into a large bowl.

11. Pour dressing on top and stir.

12. Heat a small non-stick frying pan on medium heat. Add the pumpkin seeds to the hot pan. Watch carefully, stir occasionally. When the pumpkin seeds start to "pop" and smell delicious, they are ready. Allow them to cool and then add them to your salad.

13. Serve immediately. Salad keeps well, except for the pumpkin seeds—which get soggy—so keep the roasted pumpkin seeds on the side and add as you go.

MOTHER GOOSE MIX UP

Try mint or basil instead of cilantro. And, if you can't find aji verde, use another mild pepper like banana pepper or something spicy like jalapeño if your family can handle the heat!

NUTRITION NIBBLE Long considered to be a boring diet food, celery has a lot more to offer than just its low calorie count. Celery is high in antioxidants, supports digestion, reduces inflammation, and is a good source of vitamins and minerals. Plus, celery is 95% water and can contribute to your child's fluid needs each day...think of celery as water they can crunch!

CELERY SLAW

Makes: 5 cups

Contains: None of the Common Allergens

Diet Type: Gluten Free, Dairy Free

Challenge Level: Piece of Cake

Active Time: 15 minutes

Total Time: 30 minutes

INGREDIENTS

- 2 large ripe tomatoes
- 1 large celery stalk
- ½ red or green bell pepper
- 1 small sweet onion
  (*Tip: Yellow onions are the sweetest*)
- 1 to 2 handfuls fresh parsley or cilantro
- 2 tablespoons extra virgin olive oil
- 2 tablespoons white wine vinegar
- 1 tablespoon granulated sugar
- ½ teaspoon salt
- ½ teaspoon black pepper

KIDS CAN

- Learn different knife cuts with supervision
- Wash and dry veggies
- Separate stems from leaves

WATCH OUT FOR

- Even kid-friendly knives can be sharp. Guide your child's hands as he or she chops the ingredients for this salad.

INSTRUCTIONS

1. Wash veggies and pat dry.
2. Cut the tomato, celery and bell pepper into matchsticks (julienne cut).
3. Finely slice the onion.
4. Remove leaves from parsley (or cilantro) and discard the stems.
   Finely chop the leaves (you should have about 2 tablespoons chopped).
5. Toss together all the slaw ingredients in a large bowl. Refrigerate or serve at room temperature.
   (*Tip: This is a great "make ahead" recipe. The slaw is even better the next day.*)

OLD KING COLE

OLD KING COLE

Old King Cole was a merry old soul
And a merry old soul was he;
He called for his pipe, and he called for his bowl
And he called for his fiddlers three.
Every fiddler he had a fiddle,
And a very fine fiddle had he;
Oh there's none so rare, as can compare
With King Cole and his fiddlers three!

NUTRITION NIBBLE Think of coleslaw as a "gateway salad" that opens little minds to other "salad-y" foods. Finely shred the carrots and cabbage to make this salad one kids can eat with a fork or spoon. Cabbage and tangerines are high in vitamin C. Since vitamin C helps form and repair red blood cells, bones, and tissues, eating foods like coleslaw helps minimize bruising from falls and scrapes—injuries growing children seem to have in abundance. In addition, vitamin C helps cuts and wounds heal, keeps gums healthy and keeps infections at bay. Who would have thought a salad could be so mighty!

KING COLE'S SLAW

Makes: 4 cups

Contains: Egg

Diet Type: Gluten Free, Dairy Free

Challenge Level: Piece of Cake

Active Time: 20 minutes

Total Time: 30 minutes

INGREDIENTS

For the Dressing:

- ⅓ cup mayonnaise
- ¼ cup white wine vinegar
- 2 tablespoons granulated sugar
- 1 teaspoon salt
- 1 teaspoon garlic powder
- 1 teaspoon black pepper

For the Salad:

- 1½ cups shredded green cabbage
- 1½ cups shredded purple cabbage
- 1 cup shredded carrot
- 1 granny smith apple, julienne cut
- ½ medium yellow onion, diced
- Wedges of 2 to 3 tangerines plus zest of 1

KIDS CAN

- Name the colors they see (Purple, green, white and orange)
- Whisk the dressing
- Mix in the cabbage and carrots

WATCH OUT FOR

- Kids loving cabbage
- Smaller and finer pieces are easier for younger children to chew

INSTRUCTIONS

1. Combine dressing ingredients in a small bowl and whisk until sugar is dissolved.
2. In a large bowl, mix the salad ingredients together with your clean hands.
3. Pour dressing on top, toss or stir to combine.
4. Serve immediately or chill for 15 minutes before serving for optimal flavor.

   (***Tip:*** *The longer the dressing sits on the cabbage the better the salad will taste.*)

MOTHER GOOSE MIX UP King Cole's Slaw tastes great on its own or inside sandwiches filled with **Tom's Pulled Pork** (p. 321)

HEY DIDDLE DIDDLE

HEY DIDDLE DIDDLE

Hey Diddle Diddle,

The cat and the fiddle,

The cow jumped over the moon.

The little dog laughed,

To see such sport,

And the dish ran away with the spoon.

The first time I set gooey Easy Cream Spinach out for my family, I was almost giddy. I thought this easy recipe was sure to impress. Here was the moment my kids would dig spinach. Nope. They wouldn't even try it. Pride always comes before a fall, right? Todd at least, was happy to eat their share. Well 10 (yes ten!) times after setting this dish on the dinner table, Axel and Rex finally tasted it. And they decided it was "so yum!" Sure, now there's a little less for me and Todd to enjoy, but staying persistent and modeling behavior turned a lost dish to a runaway hit.

NUTRITION NIBBLE

Nutrition research tells us that children may need exposure to a new food up to 20 times before they accept it. Kids are also little copycats, so it's important that they see you trying new foods too. One thing I've found is that when serving new foods, patience works better than pressure. This is a hard one to remember after we work hard to prepare a meal for our family—but time and time again the patient parent beats the pushy or impatient parent. I can't guarantee your children will like every new food, we all have our personal tastes, but a patient, persistent approach—and modeling an open attitude to new foods—will result in a more balanced, varied, and, dare I say, TASTY diet.

EASY CREAM SPINACH

Makes: 1½ cups
Contains: Milk
Diet Type: Gluten Free

Challenge Level: Piece of Cake
Active Time: 15 minutes
Total Time: 30 minutes

INGREDIENTS

- 6 cups fresh spinach
- 2 tablespoons unsalted butter
- 2 garlic cloves, minced
- ½ medium purple onion, diced
- 6 ounces cream cheese (about ¾ packet), cut into 3 sections
- 2 tablespoons grated Parmesan cheese

KIDS CAN

- Wash and spin the spinach
- Search for ingredients on the counter and in the refrigerator
- Sprinkle Parmesan cheese

WATCH OUT FOR

- Hot stove
- Negative attitudes

INSTRUCTIONS

1. Wash spinach and spin dry, dice onion and mince garlic.
2. Set a large deep pot or wok on medium heat.
3. Add butter, garlic and onions. Stir and cook 2 to 3 minutes. The onion should be a little crunchy but not raw.
4. Add the spinach a few handfuls at a time, stirring it around as it wilts. Cook about 2 minutes, until volume has reduced by half.
5. Add in cream cheese. Stir and mash constantly until cream cheese melts into the spinach. Sprinkle Parmesan on top.
6. Serve several ways: warm in a dish with a spoon, as a dip or rolled inside a whole grain wrap.

MOTHER GOOSE MIX UP

Take your **Easy Cream Spinach** side dish to main dish status by serving it mixed into fresh cooked pasta. Boost the nutrition even more by adding slices of grilled chicken, flakes of smoked salmon or strips of grilled steak.

LITTLE BOY BLUE

LITTLE BOY BLUE

Little Boy Blue, come blow your horn,

The sheep's in the meadow, the cow's in the corn.

But where is the boy, who looks after the sheep?

He's under a haystack, he's fast asleep.

Will you wake him? No, not I,

For if I do, he's sure to cry.

LITTLE BOY BLUE'S SAVORY AND SWEET SALADS

We refer to some foods as if they had human body parts, and it's fun to teach
these terms to our kids. Axel gets a case of the sillies when we talk about ears of corn.
He gets caught in a giggle loop holding corn next to his ears and pretending he is
listening to me. Next time you're at the supermarket, point out all the foods with
"body parts" like: fingerling potatoes or heads of cabbage, broccoli, cauliflower and garlic.
Don't forget crookneck squash, artichoke hearts, kidney beans and elbow macaroni.

NUTRITION NIBBLE Corn is a delicious and versatile whole grain that contains valuable B vitamins, which are important for overall health. Corn also provides our bodies with essential minerals such as zinc, magnesium, copper, iron and manganese. The golden kernels of corn are a good source of the antioxidants carotenoids, lutein and zeaxanthin, which promote eye health.

BLUEBERRY CORN SALAD

Makes: 5 cups
Contains: Milk
Diet Type: Gluten Free

Challenge Level: Piece of Cake
Active Time: 30 minutes
Total Time: 1 hour (includes cooling time)

INGREDIENTS

For the Salad:
- 8 medium ears sweet corn
- 1 to 2 cups fresh blueberries
- ½ cup feta cheese

For the Dressing:
- 3 tablespoons Meyer lemon infused olive oil or extra virgin olive oil
- 3 tablespoons white balsamic vinegar
- 1 handful fresh chives, cut into tiny pieces
- ¾ teaspoon salt
- Generous shake of ground pepper

KIDS CAN
- Shuck corn
- Whisk dressing
- Wash blueberries and pat dry
- Crumble feta cheese

WATCH OUT FOR
- Sharp knives

INSTRUCTIONS

1. Pull off corn husks and remove silks.
2. Cut corn from cob.
3. Toast kernels in a dry skillet on medium heat until tender and a little charred, about 20 minutes.
   (**Tip:** *Turn corn often, while some charring is nice, you don't want it to burn*).
4. Set corn aside to cool.
5. In a small bowl, whisk together oil, vinegar, chives, salt and pepper. Taste. Add lemon juice if too sweet or a pinch of sugar if too acidic.
6. Set out a large bowl and fill with cool, toasted corn.
7. Pour dressing on corn and stir.
8. Wash blueberries and pat dry, then stir them into the salad.
9. Crumble in the feta cheese and stir to incorporate.

NUTRITION NIBBLE The pomegranate is a sweet, crunchy fruit that contains hundreds of edible seeds. The seeds are rich in fiber, vitamins, minerals and bioactive plant compounds that make this tiny fruit a superfood. Recent research suggests pomegranates may have anti-aging properties as well (good for Mom and Dad!).

MANGO POMEGRANATE SALAD

Makes: 3 cups

Contains: Milk

Diet Type: Gluten Free

Challenge Level: Piece of Cake

Active Time: 45 minutes

Total Time: 45 minutes

INGREDIENTS

- Dressing from **Blueberry Corn Salad** (p. 301)
- 10 ounces fresh cut mango cubes
- 1 cup pomegranate seeds
- ½ cup crumbled feta cheese
- 4 large basil leaves cut to chiffonade

KIDS CAN

- Watch basil and spin dry
- Whisk dressing
- Crumble feta

WATCH OUT FOR

- Pomegranate juice can stain clothes. Wear an apron!

INSTRUCTIONS

1. This is simple: combine salad ingredients in a large bowl and stir in dressing!
2. Serve chilled.

MOTHER GOOSE COOKING TIP

The easiest way to seed a pomegranate is underwater. Fill a bowl with water, top and tail the pomegranate, and score along the sides. Tear open the flesh and dunk underwater. Use your fingers to loosen the seeds. The thick skin and white flesh that surrounds the seeds float, while the edible fruit sinks to the bottom of the bowl. When you're finished, skim the top of the bowl, discard the inedible portions, and strain the water.

CHAPTER 6

All the Meats

Recipes on the following pages will hopefully inspire you within the wonderful world of animal-based proteins. Animal food is the best dietary source of B12, an essential nutrient your body cannot make. You'll find new ideas for chicken (a staple food in most kids' diets) and plenty of tasty recipes to incorporate more fish and seafood into your weekly routine. Since it is recommended to consume red meat—like beef and pork—less frequently, I've included just a few of our most favorite recipes.

Around five-years-old, children can start to cut food with a knife. Fish is perfect for practicing this developmental skill because fish is soft and flakes easily. It's not until around the age of seven that most kids can use a knife and fork together to cut their meat, so be prepared to lend a helping hand. Luckily, you can eat the **Muffuletta** (p. 365) and **Sit On It Tuna Niçoise sandwiches** (p. 371), **Sweet and Sour Drumsticks** (p. 325) and **Jamaican Jerk Wings** (p. 339) with your fingers, so everyone can chow down with ease.

SING A SONG OF SIXPENCE

SING A SONG OF SIXPENCE

Sing a song of sixpence,
A pocket full of rye,
Four and twenty blackbirds
Baked in a pie.

When the pie was opened
The birds began to sing—
Wasn't that a dainty dish
To set before the King?

The King was in the counting-house
Counting out his money,
The Queen was in the parlor
Eating bread and honey.

The maid was in the garden
Hanging out the clothes.
Along came a blackbird
And snipped off her nose.

NUTRITION NIBBLE

Iron is a mineral that babies, toddlers and school-aged children need in their diet for normal growth and development. Four- to eight-year-olds should consume 10 milligrams of iron almost daily This requirement is easy to meet as long as your child eats a variety of foods. Meeting benchmarks for micronutrients like iron is trickier with picky eaters who may get the majority of their calories from fruit and dairy (which should be limited to three cups a day). The ground beef and raisins in this meat pie are good sources of iron that most kids love, plus cooking in a cast iron skillet adds iron to your food and into your body.

KING'S MEAT PIE

Makes: 10-inch pie or 12 slices

Contains: Milk, Wheat

Challenge Level: So Worth the Effort

Active Time: 1 hour 30 minutes

Total Time: 2 hours 15 minutes

This recipe is inspired by the empanada de pino, which is an individual, handheld meat pie. While living in South America, we found them just about everywhere—from kitchens, to street vendors, all the way up to the Presidential Palace. The filling for this pie is a fragrant blend of meats, spices and raisins. When you make this dish, keep in mind no pie will ever be flawless. So, don't worry if your dough doesn't roll out into a perfect circle if part of your crimp opens, or if a small portion of your pastry shrinks and slumps down. Once you slice it, no one will ever know. Trust me, I've served plenty of "imperfect" pies and have never once heard a complaint.

INGREDIENTS

For the Pastry:

- 2½ cups all-purpose flour
- 1 teaspoon salt
- 6 tablespoons unsalted butter (straight-from-the-fridge-cold)
- ¾ cup (12 tablespoons) lard
- 3 tablespoons (or up to ½ cup cold filtered water)
- 2 tablespoons almond flour for pie assembly

For the Meat Filling:

- 1 teaspoon ghee (or fat of choice)
- 1½ pounds lean ground beef
- 1 medium onion, diced
- ½ teaspoon black pepper
- ½ cup low-sodium or unsalted tomato sauce
- ½ cup ketchup
- ½ teaspoon ground cumin
- 2 teaspoons ground paprika
- ½ teaspoon granulated sugar
- 5 black olives
- ⅓ cup black raisins

KIDS CAN

- Roll out the pie dough
- "Steal" some raisins

WATCH OUT FOR

- Perfectionism (see note in the intro)

INSTRUCTIONS ON NEXT PAGE

INSTRUCTIONS

For the Pastry:

1. Cut cold butter into small cubes. In a large bowl combine salt, flour, butter and lard. Pinch and knead until a crumbly dough begins to form.

2. Add cold water 1 tablespoon at a time (up to ½ cup) until dough comes together.

3. Divide dough in half and shape each into a disc. Wrap each disc in plastic wrap and refrigerate for 1 hour or up to 2 days ahead.

For the Filling:

4. Warm a cast iron skillet on medium heat on your stove.

5. Mix tomato sauce, ketchup and seasonings together in a medium bowl.

6. Go back to your skillet and add ghee. Move it around to coat the pan.

7. Add onions, then 5 minutes later, add the ground meat. Stir meat around.

8. 5 to 10 minutes later add tomato sauce and ketchup.

9. Continue to simmer until the meat is brown.

10. Stir in the olives and raisins. Allow seasoned meat to cool before filling the pie.

KING'S MEAT PIE

INSTRUCTIONS

To Assemble:

1. Take out a 10-inch pie plate. Remove one disc of pastry from the fridge about 15 minutes before you want to roll it. Save the other disc for Step 9.

2. Test the dough in your hands by gently bending it back and forth. If it is pliable and flexible, you are ready to roll. If the dough cracks or crumbles when you bend it, wait for it to warm a little more.

3. Use a pastry mat and rolling pin to roll the first disc into a circle. Roll from the center out and avoid rolling the pin off the edge of the dough until the very end. Aim for a circle that is 3 inches larger than your pie plate.

   > **YOU DON'T HAVE TO PAINT THE PIE PLATE WITH BUTTER, THE CRUST WON'T STICK TO THE PLATE.**

4. Transition your pastry from the rolling pin to the pie plate, taking care not to break the crust.

5. Lift pastry so it falls into the pie plate to fit the corners, bottom and sides. Press pastry into the side of the plate with your fingers to form a wall.

6. Roll your pin over the top of the pie plate to cut the pastry dough that is hanging over. Use a small knife to neaten up the edges. (Alternatively, you can fold down overhanging pastry to make a decorative border.)

7. Sprinkle almond flour on top of the first crust. This will help absorb some of the filling liquid and prevent the bottom crust from going soggy.

8. Scoop in meat filling. Place in the refrigerator for 10 to 15 minutes.

9. Take out the second disc of pastry and repeat steps 2 and 3, but this time roll out the second disc to a circle just 2 inches bigger than the pie plate.

10. Repeat step 4. Press around the inside of the top edge gently with your fingers to join the top and bottom.

11. Cut 3 or 4 slits in the top crust to vent steam.

12. Preheat the oven to 350°F, convection bake.

13. Use scraps to make decorations, like feathers, on top of your pie. (***Tip:*** *use milk to "glue" the decorative feathers to the top of the pie.*)

14. Bake for 30 to 40 minutes or until the crust is golden and flaky.

JACK AND JILL

JACK AND JILL

Jack and Jill went up the hill,
To fetch a pail of water;
Jack fell down and broke his crown,
And Jill came tumbling after.

Jack got up and home did trot,
As fast as he could caper;
To old Dame Dob, who patched his nob,
With vinegar and brown paper.

Beef is a popular dinner staple in many parts of the world and this steak is one of Axel's favorite meals. We get a meat delivery from happy, grass-fed cows a couple of times a month, which makes red meat a special occasion food in our family. I make this dinner every time we get a delivery (like I said, it's Axel's favorite). The sweet-tart flavor of balsamic vinegar in the marinade and 30-minute active cooking time makes this dinner simple and "that" is a special occasion worth celebrating!

BALSAMIC SALT MARINADE

To make **Balsamic Salt** you need ½ cup coarse sea salt, 1 teaspoon dried basil, 1 teaspoon balsamic vinegar. Put ingredients in a food processor and pulse until combined. Transfer to a baking sheet and allow to dry overnight or in the oven set at a low temperature. You will have lots of salt left over. Store it in a glass jar and use it in place of plain salt whenever you're feeling "fancy."

SALT  VINEGAR STEAK

Makes: 1 steak (serve 3 to 4 ounces per person)

Contains: None of the Common Allergens

Diet Type: Gluten Free, Dairy Free

Challenge Level: Just a Pinch Involved

Active Time: 30 minutes

Total Time: 2 hours 30 minutes (includes time to marinate)

INGREDIENTS

- 6 tablespoons extra virgin olive oil, divided
- 4 tablespoons balsamic vinegar
- 2 teaspoons minced garlic
- 1 chopped rosemary sprig
- Balsamic Salt (opposite page) and pepper to taste
- T-bone steak (about 2 inches thick)

KIDS CAN

- Mix marinade
- Set the timer

WATCH OUT FOR

- Hot skillet
- Hot oven
- Wash hands with soap and water after handling raw meat

INSTRUCTIONS

1. Make a marinade by mixing 4 tablespoons of extra virgin olive oil and all of the balsamic vinegar, rosemary, and garlic in a small bowl.

2. Season steaks with salt and pepper, then place them in a resealable plastic bag with the marinade and place in the refrigerator for up to 2 hours. (**Tip:** *Sometimes resealable bags have tiny holes, so I put my bag of marinating meat in a dish before placing it in the refrigerator*).

3. Before grilling the steaks, transfer them from the bag in the fridge to a baking dish. Discard the bag of marinade.

4. Preheat oven to 425°F. Turn on the stove and heat your cast iron skillet with enough olive oil to cover the bottom (about 1 tablespoon). You are preparing to sear the steak in your skillet before finishing it in the oven.

5. When the olive oil is shimmering and the skillet is medium hot, place the steak in the skillet. Step back until the initial sizzle quiets down.

6. Drizzle remaining 1 tablespoon of olive oil on the topside of the steak. Grab some balsamic salt and use your fingers to rub it into the meat. (This is why you need a thick steak!) Finish with a few shakes of black pepper.

7. Cook steak over medium-high heat until nicely charred on the top and bottom, about 5 minutes per side.

8. Transfer the skillet to the oven. Roast for 30 minutes or until an instant-read thermometer inserted into the thickest section registers 135°F for medium rare. (**Tip:** *Start checking on meat temperature after 20 minutes in the oven.*)

9. Place the steak on a cutting board and let it rest for 10 minutes before carving.

10. For the most tender meat, slice steak against the grain. Serve immediately with **Cauliflower Purée** (p. 317).

NUTRITION NIBBLE

Often, parents are confused by how much meat their children should be eating. First, let's clarify a few vocabulary words: processed meat and red meat. Processed meat (bacon, ham, sausages and beef jerky) is transformed through methods such as salting, curing and fermentation. According to American Institute of Cancer Research, we should limit processed meats in our diets. Red meat refers to lean muscle meat including beef, pork, veal, lamb and mutton. Lean red meat is a vital source of protein, iron, zinc and vitamin B12. Eating 3 to 4 ounces of red meat (preferably grass-fed) once a week is enough to benefit from the nutrients in this food.

ALMOND CAULIFLOWER PURÉE

Makes: 3 cups

Contains: Milk, Tree Nuts

Diet Type: Gluten Free

Challenge Level: Piece of Cake

Active Time: 30 minutes

Total Time: 30 minutes

INGREDIENTS

- 1 large (6-inch diameter) head cauliflower
- ¾ cup cream
- 2 to 4 tablespoons water
- 2 handfuls (or ½ cup) blanched whole almonds
- ¼ teaspoon allspice
- 1 tablespoon unsalted butter
- 1 tablespoon granulated sugar
- Pinch of sea salt

KIDS CAN

- Scrub cauliflower
- Grab and measure almonds

WATCH OUT FOR

- Hot saucepan
- Sharp blades of the blender

INSTRUCTIONS

1. Wash cauliflower and separate into florets. A large head will typically yield 4 cups of florets.
2. Combine florets in a large, deep saucepan with cream, water, almonds and allspice.
3. Bring to a boil over medium-high heat, then reduce heat to a simmer.
4. Add butter and salt. Cover pan and simmer, stirring occasionally until tender, about 10 minutes.
5. Transfer the contents of the saucepan to a blender, in batches if necessary, and purée.
6. Add sugar. Continue to blend until smooth.
7. Serve as you would a potato purée or other side dish.

TOM, TOM, THE PIPER'S SON

Tom, Tom, the Piper's Son

Tom, Tom, the piper's son,
Stole a pig and away he run.
Tom run here, Tom run there,
Tom run through the village square.

I CHOOSE CATTLEMEN'S KANSAS CITY CLASSIC BBQ SAUCE BECAUSE IT TASTES GREAT, IS GLUTEN FREE AND DOES NOT CONTAIN ANY OF THE EIGHT COMMON ALLERGENS.

NUTRITION NIBBLE Pork is an animal protein and adds variety to the typical fish, chicken and beef rotation. It is a good source of many vitamins and minerals—too many to list right here. What's more, pork contains more thiamine (one of the B vitamins) than other red meats, and while it has less iron than other red meats, it's iron is as easy to absorb, making it an excellent source for this important mineral.

TOM'S PULLED PORK

Makes:	3 pounds (serve 3 to 4 ounces per person)	**Challenge Level:**	Piece of Cake
Contains:	None of the Common Allergens	**Active Time:**	15 minutes
Diet Type:	Gluten Free, Dairy Free	**Total Time:**	4 hours 15 minutes (includes 4 hours in the slow cooker)

I love my slow cooker—there is not a woman in my family who doesn't have one. It's my best kitchen friend next to the coffee pot. The "set it and forget it" slogan jives with my lazy inner cook. (And I never have to compromise on flavor!) Pulled pork is simply slow-cooked pork roast pulled into shreds and mixed with barbecue sauce and its own juices before serving. Whenever we visit the grandparents, you can be sure this is the first meal we eat. By the time we have napped from our overnight flight, showered and unpacked our bags, lunch is ready.

INGREDIENTS

- ¾ cup gluten-free barbecue sauce
- 3 tablespoons tomato paste
- ¼ cup apple cider vinegar
- 1 teaspoon paprika
- 1 teaspoon garlic powder
- 1 teaspoon onion powder
- 1 teaspoon mustard powder
- 1 teaspoon cumin
- 1 (3 to 4 pounds) frozen boneless pork shoulder

KIDS CAN

- Measure, sprinkle and stir seasonings
- Pour the liquid ingredients, stir the marinade
- Push the buttons on the slow cooker with supervision
- Help make pork sandwiches

WATCH OUT FOR

- Wash hands with soap and water after handling raw meat
- Hot sides of the slow cooker

INSTRUCTIONS

1. Combine sauce, tomato paste, apple cider vinegar and spices in the bowl of a slow cooker. Add pork (fatty side up) and stir to coat it all over with the sauce mixture.
2. Put the lid on the slow cooker and set to high heat for 3 to 4 hours—less time if using defrosted pork. When the meat falls apart easily with a fork, it is ready.
3. Shred the pork with two forks directly in the slow cooker (careful not to touch the hot sides), or transfer to a new bowl first and then shred.
4. Toss the shredded pork with the juices that remain in the slow cooker.
5. Serve on sandwiches made with **King Cole's Slaw** (p. 293), mix shredded pork inside **Silver Spoonbread** (p. 149) or simply eat with a fork.

AIKEN DRUM

AIKEN DRUM

There was a man lived in the moon, lived in the moon, lived in the moon,
There was a man lived in the moon,
And his name was Aiken Drum.

(Chorus) And he played upon a ladle, a ladle, a ladle,
And he played upon a ladle,
and his name was Aiken Drum.

And his hat was made of celery slaw, of celery slaw, of **Celery Slaw**,
And his hat was made of celery slaw,
And his name was Aiken Drum.

~ Chorus ~

And his coat was made of king's meat pie, of king's meat pie, of **King's Meat Pie**,
And his coat was made of king's meat pie,
And his name was Aiken Drum.

~ Chorus ~

And his buttons were made of cinnamon rolls, of cinnamon rolls, of **Cinnamon Rolls**,
And his buttons were made of cinnamon rolls,
And his name was Aiken Drum.

~ Chorus ~

And his socks were made of honey peas, of honey peas, of **Honey Peas**,
And his socks were made of honey peas,
And his name was Aiken Drum.

~ Chorus ~

And his boots were made of truffle fries, of truffle fries, of **Truffle Fries**,
And his boots were made of truffle fries
And his name was Aiken Drum.

~ Chorus ~

323

USING A CERTIFIED GLUTEN-FREE BRAND
LIKE KIKKOMAN GLUTEN-FREE TAMARI SAUCE
MAKES THIS RECIPE SAFE FOR FAMILIES
FOLLOWING A GLUTEN-FREE DIET

NUTRITION NIBBLE Some people avoid dark chicken meat, while others will eat nothing else. So, what is the difference between white meat and dark meat, anyway? Without getting too scientific, dark meat contains myoglobin, the hemoprotein (an oxygen-carrying protein) responsible for giving dark meat its color. The more myoglobin, the darker the meat and the richer the nutrients. While dark meat is higher in saturated fat than white meat, the difference is not as much as you may think (and the extra fat gives drumsticks their juicy flavor). Any way you take it, chicken is good for you—both white and dark meat are excellent sources of protein, niacin, phosphorous, B6, B12, Vitamin D, calcium, iron and zinc. Chicken legs (drumsticks) are ideal for kids who love to pick up their food. So go ahead and add a little dark meat to the menu.

SWEET AND SOUR DRUMSTICKS

Makes:	6 drumsticks, plus extra sauce	**Challenge Level:**	Piece of Cake
Contains:	Wheat, Soy	**Active Time:**	45 minutes
Diet Type:	Gluten Free option, Dairy Free	**Total Time:**	1 hour 30 minutes (includes 30-minute marinade)

INGREDIENTS

- 6 drumsticks

For the Marinade and Sauce:
- 4 tablespoons low sodium soy or tamari sauce
- 4 tablespoons honey
- 1 finger (about 1 tablespoon) ginger, grated
- 3 cloves garlic, minced
- Pinch of red pepper flakes, optional but recommended
- 2 teaspoons dark sesame oil
- 1 tablespoon mirin or rice vinegar
- 3 shakes of sesame seeds, lightly toasted as a garnish, more as desired
- 1 green onion finely sliced as a garnish

KIDS CAN

- Look for the ingredients in the kitchen
- Set the timer
- Sprinkle the sesame seeds
- Garnish chicken with sliced scallions
- Eat with their fingers

WATCH OUT FOR

- Wash hands after touching raw chicken

INSTRUCTIONS

1. Combine all marinade ingredients in a bowl. Whisk vigorously.
2. If you have time to marinate the chicken, it's better. Place the chicken and half the marinade in a resealable plastic bag. Refrigerate for about 30 minutes or up to 2 hours. (***Tip:*** *Sometimes resealable bags have tiny holes, so I put my bag of marinating chicken in a dish before placing it in the refrigerator.*)
3. Reserve remaining marinade for the glaze.
4. When ready to bake, set the oven to 425°F. Place marinated chicken and accumulated juices in a single layer on a rimmed baking sheet lined with parchment paper.
5. Bake approximately 40 minutes, flipping the drumsticks halfway through. Dark meat is best cooked to the point that it has begun to shrink away from the bone; which is way past the point of it having reached a safe temperature. (To be certain, use a thermometer to check that the internal temperature is 165°F.)
6. While the chicken is cooking, place the reserved marinade in a saucepan and gently simmer, stirring occasionally. The marinade will thicken to a glaze in about 15 minutes.
   (***Tip:*** *To know when the glaze is ready, use the "spoon test". Note that glaze continues to thicken as it cools.*)
7. Pour glaze over the wings and garnish with sesame seeds and green onion.

DIDDLE, DIDDLE DUMPLING

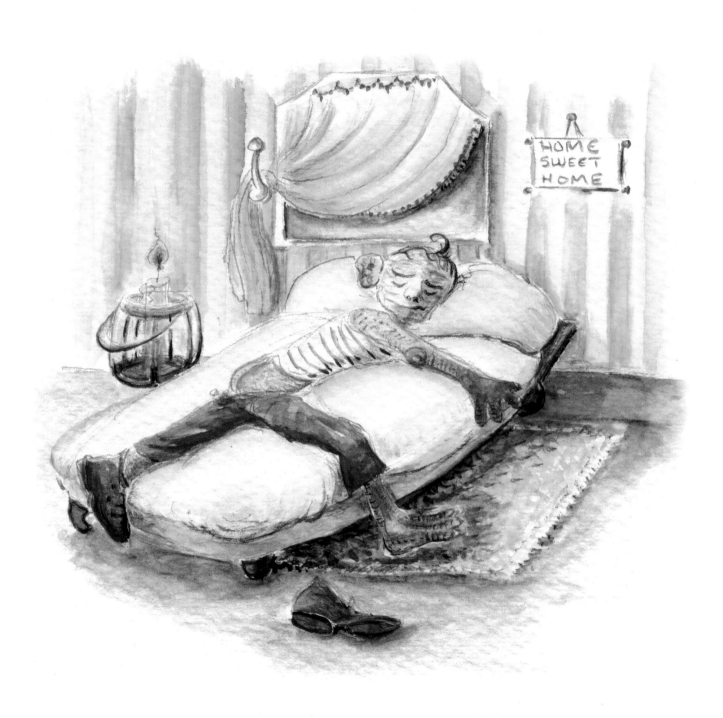

DIDDLE, DIDDLE DUMPLING

Diddle, diddle dumpling, my son John,
Went to bed with his breeches on,
One stocking off and one stocking on,
Diddle, diddle dumpling my son John.

These Diddle Dumplings are my take on traditional chicken and dumplings. It's a real comfort food in my home and—the best part—it's as easy to prepare as it is to enjoy. Because stressing over comfort food sort of defeats the purpose, right? As soon as the chopping board comes out, I know my little ones are bound to peek their heads in to see what Mom is up to. They want to explore the smells and sights (and snatch a carrot or two before I get to chopping). Thankfully, this recipe is so user-friendly it's nearly impossible to mess up—no matter what you have on hand. Got frozen corn lying around? Toss it in! Peas? Go for it, mama! Even if you step away from the stove for a minute to chase your little carrot thief, not a problem. This is a great recipe to experiment with and let your child help. The result: a savory, hearty classic that will warm you from the inside out.

WHEN YOUR SOUP IS SIMMERING IT'S TIME FOR THE FUN PART!
MAKING THE DIDDLE DUMPLINGS! HAVE YOUR CHILD WASH THEIR
HANDS AND KNEAD THE DOUGH FOR A FUN SENSORY EXPERIENCE.

NUTRITION NIBBLE   Balance is the name of the game with this recipe. Carbs, healthy fats and proteins are all well represented. And it's an excellent opportunity to throw in lots of veggies.

CHICKEN  DUMPLINGS

Makes: 5 cups	**Challenge Level:** Piece of Cake
Contains: Milk, Wheat	**Active Time:** 30 minutes
	Total Time: 1 hour

INGREDIENTS

For the Stew:

- 12 ounces cooked chicken breast (the white meat from store-bought rotisserie works well)
- 2 medium carrots
- 1 purple onion
- 2 medium celery stalks with leaves
- 2 tablespoons unsalted butter
- ¼ cup all-purpose flour
- 4 cups **Chicken Stock** (p. 63) or use store-bought
- ½ teaspoon ground white pepper
- ½ cup buttermilk

For the Dumplings:

- 1 cup of all-purpose flour
- ½ teaspoon salt
- 1 teaspoon baking powder
- ½ teaspoon dried marjoram
- ½ teaspoon dried thyme
- ½ teaspoon dried oregano
- 2 tablespoons unsalted butter, melted
- ½ cup buttermilk

KIDS CAN

- Wash and dry vegetables
- Peel the carrots with help
- Sprinkle in seasonings
- Mix ingredients to form the dumpling dough
- Spray the tablespoon

WATCH OUT FOR

- Simmering soup and sharp objects.

INSTRUCTIONS ON NEXT PAGE

CHICKEN AND DUMPLINGS CONTINUED

INSTRUCTIONS

For the Stew:

1. Remove meat from the bones of a store-bought rotisserie chicken. Discard the skin. (Skip if using baked chicken breasts). Tear or cut chicken into big bite size pieces, then set aside.
2. Wash your veggies and pat dry. Peel the carrots. Chop the onion, celery and carrots to a small dice.
3. Place a deep pot on the stove and set to medium heat. Toss in butter and, once melted, add the veggies and cook until they start to soften (about 5 minutes).
4. Add flour and stir to coat the veggies. Add white pepper.
5. Immediately pour in the stock and bring to a boil.
6. Add chicken and buttermilk and turn heat down to a simmer while you make the dumpling dough. (Dumpling dough takes about 15 minutes to prepare.)

For the Dumplings:

7. Add all dumpling ingredients to a mixing bowl.
8. Use your hands (or a fork) to stir and make a ball of dough. Don't overwork it or the dumplings won't be pillowy.
9. Spray a tablespoon with cooking spray (this makes it easier for the dumplings to slide out). Carefully drop dumpling dough by the spoonful into the simmering pot. Add enough dumplings to cover the top of the pot—you don't want dumplings to touch each other.
10. Cover the pot and reduce heat to low for 15 minutes. Make sure not to open the pot to peek as the dumplings need the steam to cook and fluff up.
11. After 15 minutes, turn off the heat. If you are ready to serve, go ahead, if not, leave it on the stove, covered (remember no peeking!) for up to 30 minutes while you set the table, wash hands and generally get ready for dinner. At this point, the consistency is like a stew or thick gravy—the ultimate comfort food texture! Serve in a bowl or deep plate.

LITTLE JACK HORNER

LITTLE JACK HORNER

Little Jack Horner
Sat in a corner,
Eating a Christmas pie.
He stuck in his thumb
And pulled out a plum,
And said, "What a good boy am I!"

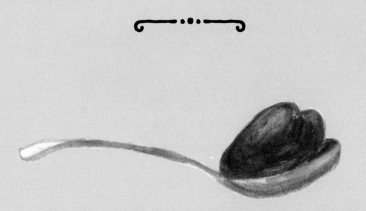

I'm a big fan of one-dish meals. What's better on a busy weeknight than a fuss-free recipe that's full of delicious ingredients? Throw everything in a skillet, let it cook and dinner is done. With just one pan to clean, you can sit back, relax and read more nursery rhymes together. The sweetness of the plums and complexity of the ginger and soy glaze make this chicken as easy to eat as it is to make. So go ahead Mama, and give yourself two thumbs up!

CHICKEN AND PLUM SKILLET

Makes: About 4 cups (serve 1 cup per person)	**Challenge Level:** Piece of Cake
Contains: Wheat, Soy	**Active Time:** 45 minutes
Diet Type: Dairy Free option	**Total Time:** 1 hour

INGREDIENTS

- 2 tablespoons extra virgin olive oil
- 1 tablespoon garlic and herb spice (Our family likes McCormick Perfect Pinch Garlic and Herb, salt free)
- 1 pound boneless, skinless chicken tenders
- 1 tablespoon ghee, butter or lard
- ½ purple onion, diced
- 3 or 4 fresh plums, pit removed and cut into wedges
- 1 piece fresh ginger, peeled and grated
- 1 tablespoon balsamic vinegar
- 2 tablespoons low-sodium soy sauce
- Pinch of dried thyme
- 1 tablespoon cornstarch
- 2 tablespoons white wine
- 6 tablespoons store-bought apricot marmalade

KIDS CAN

- Wash fruit and pat dry
- Whisk wine and cornstarch
- Set the timer

WATCH OUT FOR

- Sharp knives
- Hot skillet

INSTRUCTIONS

1. Place chicken tenders, garlic and herb blend and a little olive oil in a resealable plastic bag. Massage chicken through the bag and set it aside to marinate for 5 minutes.
2. Heat a large cast iron skillet over medium heat for 3 minutes.
3. Add ghee and, when it is melted, add onions and marinated tenders.
4. Cook about 10 minutes, then add plums. Continue to cook and stir for 2 minutes.
5. Reduce heat. Add ginger, balsamic, soy sauce and thyme. Stir and cook for 5 minutes so the flavors marry.
6. Whisk cornstarch and wine together to make a slurry. Pour the slurry into the skillet.
7. Add in the apricot marmalade and stir until the flavors have incorporated and plums are tender, about 10 more minutes.
8. Sprinkle with toasted sesame seeds before serving.

JACK SPRAT

JACK SPRAT

Jack Sprat could eat no fat,
His wife could eat no lean,
And so between them both,
They licked the platter clean.

Jack ate all the lean,
Joan ate all the fat;
The bone they picked clean,
Then gave it to the cat.

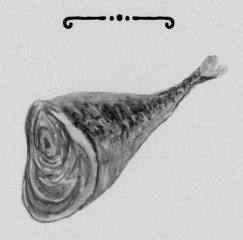

JACK SPRAT'S SMATTERINGS

Does this sound like your family: Everyone wants something different or has a different dietary restriction? This rhyme inspired recipes that offer a little something for everyone. The **Jamaican Jerk Wings** are gluten and dairy free, **Steamed Artichokes** are vegetarian (and vegan) and the **Skillet Steak Teriyaki** is a balanced one-pot meal that can be ready fast. In other words, no matter the differing preferences at your table, you'll all lick the platter clean!

JAMAICAN JERK CHICKEN WINGS

Makes: 12 wings

Contains: None of the Common Allergens

Diet Type: Gluten Free, Dairy Free

Challenge Level: Piece of Cake

Active Time: 20 minutes

Total Time: 2 hours (includes 30 minute marinade time)

INGREDIENTS

- 12 chicken wings
- ½ cup gluten-free BBQ sauce of your choice (We like Cattlemen's Kansas City Classic)

For the Jamaican Jerk Seasoning:
- 1½ tablespoons onion powder
- 1½ tablespoons garlic powder
- 1 tablespoon ground ginger
- 1 tablespoon dried thyme
- 1 teaspoon ground white pepper
- 1 tablespoon allspice
- 1 tablespoon sweet paprika
- ½ tablespoon cinnamon
- ½ tablespoon ground nutmeg
- 1 teaspoon gluten-free vegetable bouillon

KIDS CAN

- Measure spices for seasoning
- Shake or stir spices together
- Cut or tear parchment paper to line the baking sheet
- Eat with their fingers

WATCH OUT FOR

- Wash hands after touching raw chicken

INSTRUCTIONS

1. Place wings in a bowl and coat with barbecue sauce. Set aside while you make the seasoning blend.
2. Mix all the herbs and spices for the Jamaican Jerk seasoning together in a jar and stir until incorporated. Put on the lid and shake to incorporate.
3. Liberally shake, sprinkle or spoon jerk seasoning onto the BBQ-coated wings, pressing the powder into the meat with your fingertips. Wash hands with soap and water. Marinate 30 minutes or up to 2 hours.
4. Preheat oven to 320°F. Transfer wings to a baking sheet lined with parchment paper and bake for 1 hour.
5. Serve immediately. (*Tip: You'll have enough Jamaican Jerk seasoning to make a second batch of wings if friends stop by for a bite!*)

MY BOYS PREFER THEIR ARTICHOKES PURE. THEY DON'T DIP THE BRACTS IN VINAIGRETTE LIKE TODD AND I DO. SO, ALWAYS SERVE THE SAUCE ON THE SIDE.

NUTRITION NIBBLE

Although often considered a vegetable, artichokes are a type of thistle with a pretty purple flower. Artichokes are low in fat, high in fiber and loaded with vitamins and minerals like vitamin C, vitamin K, folate, phosphorus and magnesium. They are also one of the richest sources of antioxidants. The edible parts of the artichoke include the outer leaves and heart. Cooked artichokes can be eaten hot or cold, but we prefer them hot.

STEAMED ARTICHOKES ~WITH~ VINAIGRETTE

Makes: 4 artichokes	**Challenge Level:** Piece of Cake
Contains: None of the Common Allergens	**Active Time:** 20 minutes
Diet Type: Gluten Free, Dairy Free	**Total Time:** 2 hours (includes 30 minute marinade time)

Most people know that you can eat the heart of an artichoke. But, did you know the bracts (the special leaf of the artichoke) have a soft, edible part too? Pull off the outer bracts one by one, starting at the bottom, as if you were pulling petals off a flower. Put the base of each bract (the base is lighter in color) in your mouth and scrape the soft part off with your teeth. Then, grab a new one, working your way upwards and inwards. To get to the heart, cut or scrape out the fuzzy, prickly choke in the center and eat the tender heart. If you don't eat all the artichoke hearts, make **Black Bean and Artichoke Enchilada Wreath** (p. 249).

INGREDIENTS

- 4 artichokes (one for each person)

For the Vinaigrette:

- 1 small shallot, minced
- ¼ cup extra virgin olive oil
- Juice of 1 lemon (about 2 tablespoons)
- 1 tablespoon white wine vinegar
- 1 teaspoon dijon mustard
- Salt and pepper to taste

KIDS CAN

- Wash artichokes
- Set the timer
- Pull off the bracts
- Dip, scrape, eat and repeat!

WATCH OUT FOR

- Hot steam
- Piles of bracts

INSTRUCTIONS

For the Vinaigrette: This one's easy! Add all the ingredients to a jar with a tightly fitting lid. Shake jar and stop when the vinaigrette has emulsified.

For the Artichokes:

1. Fill a huge pot that holds a steamer basket with water. The water line should stop just below the bottom of the steamer basket. Bring water to a boil.
2. Aggressively wash artichokes in running water. Dirt likes to hide in the many nooks and crannies and down around the base of the bracts.
3. Trim the stems and remove the tough outer layer of bracts at the base. Trim the barbs (found at the tip of each bract) with kid-safe scissors.
4. When water is boiling, place artichokes in the steamer basket. Cover pot and set a timer for 30 minutes.
5. When timer sounds, carefully lift the lid of your pot, allowing the steam to escape. Poke the bottom part of the artichoke stem with a butter knife. If the knife enters easily, artichokes are done.
6. Remove the basket from the pot and drain over the sink until cool enough to handle.
7. Place artichokes on a platter and gently press down on top to open the bracts.
8. Serve with the vinaigrette on the side (for dipping!) and an extra plate for the bracts.

TERIYAKI STEAK SKILLET

~ • •• • ~

Makes: About 4 cups (Serve 1 cup per person)
Contains: Wheat, Soy
Diet Type: Dairy Free

Challenge Level: Piece of Cake
Active Time: 20 minutes
Total Time: 1 hour (including marinade)

INGREDIENTS

- 1½ pounds beef fillet cut into bite-size cubes
- ¾ cup low-sodium teriyaki sauce, store-bought
- 1 tablespoon extra virgin olive oil (enough to coat the bottom of your skillet)
- 1 medium onion, finely chopped
- 1 clove garlic, minced
- 1 tablespoon ginger, minced
- 2 "baby" bok choy, separate leaves and stems
- 1 handful Chinese chives (can substitute regular chives)

KIDS CAN

- Wash bok choy and pat dry
- Separate bok choy leaves from stems
- Snip chives with supervision
- Measure teriyaki sauce

WATCH OUT FOR

- Hot skillet and sharp objects

INSTRUCTIONS

1. Combine fillet and teriyaki sauce in a resealable plastic bag and, if you have time, marinate 30 minutes or up to 2 hours. (**Tip:** *No time to marinate, no problem—just massage the sauce and meat through the bag, about 5 minutes and start cooking).*
2. Roughly chop bok choy and separate the leaves and stems into two piles.
3. Heat a large cast iron skillet on medium heat, then add olive oil.
4. Sauté onion, garlic and ginger for 3 minutes.
5. Add marinated meat. Lower heat so mixture is at a low simmer. Cook together for about 5 minutes.
6. Toss in the bok choy stems. Continue for 5 more minutes, then add bok choy leaves. Cook an additional 3 minutes or until sauce thickens slightly.
7. Use kid-safe scissors to snip Chinese chives into little pieces. Sprinkle on top.
8. Serve alone, with **Whole Grain (Brown) Rice** (p. 88) or on top of cooked rice noodles.

WORMS

WORMS

Nobody likes me,
Everybody hates me,
Guess I'll go eat worms.

Long, thin, slimy ones,
Short, fat, juicy ones,
Itsy, bitsy, fuzzy wuzzy worms.

Down goes the first one,
Down goes the second one,
Oh, how they wiggle and squirm.

Up comes the first one,
Up comes the second one,
Oh, how they wiggle and squirm.

NUTRITION NIBBLE A cousin of pumpkin and zucchini, you can recognize spaghetti squash by its smooth bright-yellow skin and oval shape. It's a smart swap for noodles due to the stringy, noodle-ish texture of its flesh. Spaghetti squash is also a good source of fiber, vitamin C, manganese and vitamin B6.

SPAGHETTI SQUASH SHRIMP PAD THAI

Makes:	8 cups (serve 1 cup per person)	**Challenge Level:**	Piece of Cake
Contains:	Egg, Wheat, Shellfish, Peanuts, Soy	**Active Time:**	30 minutes
Diet Type:	Dairy Free, Gluten Free option	**Total Time:**	2 hours (includes time in slow cooker)

You may remember I mentioned the women in my family live and breathe by their slow cooker (p. 321) and this recipe wholeheartedly continues the tradition. My mom first introduced me to nutrient-dense spaghetti squash as a substitute for noodles in this peanut-y spin on shrimp pad Thai. Paired with the (admittedly icky, but still fun) rhyme, this dish was an instant hit with my littles who wiggled and squirmed as they slurped it up.

INGREDIENTS

For the "Worms" (Spaghetti Squash):
- 1 spaghetti squash
- 1 cup filtered water

For the Pad Thai Sauce:
- ⅔ cups **Chicken Stock** (p. 63)
- 2 tablespoons soy sauce (For a gluten-free option, use Kikkoman Gluten-Free Soy Sauce)
- ⅓ cup packed brown sugar
- ½ cup peanut butter
- 2 tablespoons lime juice
- 2 tablespoons mirin (or rice vinegar)
- ½ teaspoon chili pepper
- 2 teaspoons minced ginger
- 2 cloves minced garlic
- 2 green onions, sliced
- 2 limes cut in wedges
- 1 handful peanuts, roughly chopped

For the Shrimp:
- 2 teaspoons extra virgin olive oil
- 1 pound shrimp, peeled and deveined
- 1 cup bean sprouts, optional
- 2 large eggs

KIDS CAN

- Wash the spaghetti squash
- Scoop out spaghetti squash once cool
- Squeeze the limes
- Crack and beat the eggs with help
- Bash peanuts into bits for garnish

WATCH OUT FOR

- Hot pots
- Hot squash. Allow spaghetti squash to cool before scooping out the insides
- Squash seeds can be a choking hazard

INSTRUCTIONS ON NEXT PAGE

347

SPAGHETTI SQUASH SHRIMP PAD THAI

INSTRUCTIONS

For the "Worms" (Spaghetti Squash):

1. Take out your slow cooker, plug it in and set the temperature to low and the timer to 2 hours. Pour water in the bottom—enough to have about half an inch of standing water. Set the spaghetti squash inside, close the lid.

2. After 2 hours, pierce the spaghetti squash with a fork. If the fork easily passes through the skin, the squash is ready. If it doesn't, cook another 30 minutes. Cooking time depends on your slow cooker and the size of your squash. (*Tip: if you don't have a slow cooker, preheat oven to 400°F and place spaghetti squash and water in a casserole dish. Bake uncovered for about 45 minutes.*)

For the Pad Thai Sauce:

3. Place a medium-size saucepan on medium heat. Put all the sauce ingredients in the saucepan and simmer together. The flavors will combine and the peanut butter will melt.

4. Stir often and, if the sauce starts to boil, lift the pot off of the heat and set it down again when the bubbles stop. When the sauce is finished, about 5 minutes, remove from heat. Sauce will thicken as it cools.

For the Shrimp:

5. Heat olive oil in a nonstick frying pan or wok.

6. Add in fresh, peeled shrimp and sauté for 2 to 3 minutes

7. Throw in the bean sprouts (if using) and pour half of the sauce over the shrimp and sprouts.

8. In a separate bowl, beat the eggs and then pour them into the frying pan. Stir to incorporate.

9. When eggs are no longer runny, turn off the stove. This whole process takes about 7 minutes.

To Assemble:

10. Remove cooked spaghetti squash from the slow cooker. Once cool, cut the squash in half. Scoop out the seeds and discard. With a fork, pull and shred the flesh of the spaghetti squash into little noodles.

11. Combine the noodles with the shrimp mixture and remaining sauce just before serving. (**Note:** do not combine before serving because the spaghetti squash loses water over time and you don't want soggy "worms".)

12. Garnish with chopped peanuts, sliced green onion and lime wedges.

WHEN THE WIND

WHEN THE WIND

When the wind is in the east,

'Tis good for neither man nor beast;

When the wind is in the north,

The skillful fisher goes not forth;

When the wind is in the south,

It blows the bait in the fishes' mouth;

When the wind is in the west,

Then 'tis at the very best.

FISH OF THE FOUR WINDS

NUTRITION NIBBLE We have a chance to shape our children's young taste buds to actually love and crave the taste of fish! Fish is packed with nutrients for the brain and bones, such as omega-3 fatty acids and DHA, calcium and vitamin D—so don't be afraid to start serving it to your family. I created these recipes around each fish's flavor and nutrient profile, but feel free to mix and match. For example, Mahi Mahi will work great in the **Moqueca**, or swap tilapia for strips of salmon when making **Crispy Coconut Tilapia** and you've got kid-pleasing, superfood fish sticks.

MOTHER GOOSE COOKING TIP

Fishy smells are a turnoff to anyone—and for a good reason. Those odors are a sign that seafood is no longer fresh. Fish should smell briny, like the sea. Not stinky. Because seafood spoils more quickly than other meats, make sure to eat it within two days of purchase.

TERIYAKI SALMON

Makes: 2 pounds (serve 3 to 4 ounces per person)

Contains: Wheat, Fish, Soy

Diet Type: Gluten Free Option

Challenge Level: Piece of Cake

Active Time: 10 minutes

Total Time: 30 minutes

Hey Dad! This recipe is for you. My husband threw together this simple combination of sweet and tangy flavors one night when I was out of town. Boy's night could have been pizza, but instead, Todd brought home a thick salmon fillet. His four-ingredient dinner was a home run and we've been making salmon this way ever since. Todd grilled it outside on the barbecue, but I prefer baking salmon in the oven. If your kids are new to salmon, I'd start with this recipe—it's low-maintenance and healthy. Go, Dad, Go!

INGREDIENTS

- 2 pound salmon fillet, skin on and descaled
- ¼ to ½ cup teriyaki sauce (or swap for a certified gluten free teriyaki sauce)
- Zest and juice of 1 orange
- 1 finger or to taste fresh ginger, grated or diced, divided

KIDS CAN

- Make aluminum foil "boats"
- Squeeze the orange
- Press ginger into the fillet

WATCH OUT FOR

- Sharp knives
- Wash hands after handling raw fish

INSTRUCTIONS

1. Preheat oven to 275°F and line a large, rimmed baking sheet with aluminum foil.
2. Make a "boat" with the aluminum foil and place the salmon, skin side down, in the center.
3. Sprinkle half the ginger on salmon—pressing it into the fillet with your fingers.
4. Carefully pour teriyaki sauce on top, then squeeze on the orange juice and sprinkle with orange zest and the rest of the ginger.
5. Bake for 15 to 18 minutes. Salmon is done when it flakes with a fork, the internal temperature reaches 145°F or when the fish is not raw and mushy inside. (*Tip: You can also place salmon on an outdoor barbecue. In this case, cook foil-wrapped salmon on the top rack.*)
6. Salmon tastes better when cooked slowly at a lower temperature rather than quickly at a high temperature. Serve with **Long Grain White Rice** (p. 86).

MAHI MAHI BOWTIE PASTA

Makes: Makes about 6 cups

Contains: Wheat, Fish, Tree Nuts

Diet Type: Dairy Free

Challenge Level: Just a Pinch Involved

Active Time: 45 minutes

Total Time: 45 minutes

Mahi Mahi is lean with firm texture and a mild, sweet flavor. Its large, moist flakes stand up to pastas, curries and tacos. Fresh Mahi Mahi should have a translucent pinkish flesh and a bright red bloodline. Look for sources caught in the U.S. as most imported sources are on the Monterey Bay Aquarium Seafood Watch's "avoid" list.

INGREDIENTS

- 2 tablespoons extra virgin olive oil, divided
- 1 packet (16 ounces) colorful bow tie noodles
- 4 mahi mahi fillets (about 3 ounces each)
- 1 cup fresh peas
- 1 handful (¼ cup) toasted, salted Marcona almonds
- 2 cloves garlic, minced
- Zest and juice of 1 lemon
- ¼ cup flat leaf parsley, chopped fine
- Pinch of salt

KIDS CAN

- Shell the peas
- Set the timer
- Pick parsley leaves off the stem
- Grab the almonds

WATCH OUT FOR

- Sharp knives
- Wash hands after handling raw fish

INSTRUCTIONS

1. In a medium saucepan, boil water. Once boiling, add noodles and salt.
2. Set a timer for 8 minutes. Stir pasta occasionally.
3. While the pasta is cooking, start prepping the fish. Heat broiler of the oven.
4. Sprinkle both sides of fish with a drizzle of oil, salt and pepper. Place on a foil-lined baking sheet and broil 5" to 6" from heat, until fish is opaque, and flakes easily with a fork (5 minutes per ½ inch of thickness).
5. Meanwhile pull out your skillet.
6. Over low heat, warm remaining olive oil and sauté garlic in the skillet. Add ¼ cup of cooking pasta water to the skillet to prevent burning.
7. Chop parsley and almonds or pulse together in your food processor. Zest the lemon.
8. When timer goes off, taste a bowtie and check on fish.
9. Once pasta is *al dente,* add fresh peas to the pasta pot and then turn off the heat.
10. Scoop out another ¼ cup of your pasta water and set it aside in case you need it.
11. Wait 1 minute before straining pasta and peas.
12. Add peas and pasta to your warm skillet with the zest, lemon juice, chopped parsley, almonds and, if you want, the reserved pasta water.
13. Use a wide spatula to transfer the fish fillets to the skillet. Stir together allowing the fish to flake apart.
14. Mix until flavors combine, but colors remain vibrant.
15. Serve immediately or "blow-on-it-hot".

NUTRITION NIBBLE This recipe uses tilapia—an inexpensive, mildly sweet-flavored white fish widely available all over the world. Tilapia is high in several vitamins and minerals such as selenium, vitamin B12, niacin and potassium. It pairs well with fruit salsas like **Piña and Avocado Salsa** (p. 359). Due to a lack of data on environmental impact and potential for chemical use, the Monterey Bay Aquarium Seafood Watch recommends avoiding farmed tilapia from Colombia. Other white fish that work with this recipe are cod or barramundi.

CRISPY COCONUT TILAPIA

Makes: 1 pound (serve 3 to 4 ounces per person)

Contains: Egg, Wheat, Fish

Challenge Level: Just a Pinch Involved

Active Time: 30 minutes

Total Time: 30 minutes

INGREDIENTS

- 1 pound (4 to 6 fillets) tilapia
- ½ cup all-purpose flour
- ¼ teaspoon salt
- ¼ teaspoon black pepper
- 2 eggs, beaten
- 2 cups cornflakes, crushed by hand or in food processor
- ½ cup shredded coconut
- Juice of ½ lemon

KIDS CAN

- Crush cereal
- Count 3 bowls
- Beat egg
- Squeeze lemon
- Prepare a plate with paper towels

WATCH OUT FOR

- Wash hands after handling raw fish
- Oil splatters

INSTRUCTIONS

1. Lay out 3 shallow bowls.
2. In one bowl, stir together flour, salt and pepper. In the second bowl, beat 2 eggs together. In the third bowl, place crumbled corn flakes and shredded coconut.
3. Dip fish in flour, then in egg and finally dredge in cereal and coconut.
4. Preheat over to 350°F, convection bake. Liberally coat a rimmed baking sheet with canola oil and place coconut-crusted fish in a single layer. Bake 5 to 7 minutes for fish, depending on size of fillets. Fish is done when internal temperature reaches 145°F. There is no need to flip.
5. Once cooked, squeeze lemon juice over the fish.
6. Serve "blow-on-it-hot" with **Piña and Avocado Salsa** (p. 359) and store-bought Thai Sweet Chili Sauce *(**Tip:** My boys like Thai Sweet Chile mixed with ketchup so it's less "spicy")*

MOTHER GOOSE MIX UP

You can freeze leftovers in a resealable plastic bag. To reheat, set the oven to 350°F and bake for about 10 minutes, until fish is warm and crispy.

PIÑA AND AVOCADO SALSA

Makes: About 1 cup

Contains: None of the Common Allergens

Diet Type: Gluten Free, Dairy Free

Challenge Level: Piece of Cake

Active Time: 30 minutes

Total Time: 30 minutes

INGREDIENTS

- 1 ripe avocado
- 1 cup fresh or canned pineapple
- 1 green onion
- 1 to 2 tablespoons of toasted coconut flakes
- Juice of 1 lime, plus more to taste
- Handful of fresh cilantro

KIDS CAN

- Roll and squeeze the lime
- Chop avocado with help
- Wash and spin cilantro
- Separate cilantro leaves from stems
- Stir
- Learn the Spanish word for pineapple (piña)

WATCH OUT FOR

- Sharp knives for cutting the lime and avocado
- Tiny cuts on your hands will sting if lime juice gets inside

INSTRUCTIONS

1. Wash avocado. Cut the avocado in half, remove pit and scoop out the flesh. On a cutting board, chop avocado and pineapple into small cubes. Transfer to a medium bowl.
2. Mince green onion and add it to the bowl.
3. Squeeze in the lime juice.
4. Tear the leaves off the cilantro stems and rip them into smaller pieces (or cut leaves with kitchen scissors).
5. Season with salt and pepper to taste.
6. In a dry non-stick frying pan, toast a small handful of coconut flakes. Add them to the salsa just before serving.

MOQUECA STEW ⌖WITH⌖ SALMON

Makes: 8 cups (serve 1 cup per person)

Contains: Fish

Diet Type: Gluten Free, Dairy Free

Challenge Level: Piece of Cake

Active Time: 45 minutes

Total Time: 1 hour (includes 30-minute marinade time)

INGREDIENTS

For the Marinade:

- 3 large garlic cloves, minced
- 2 tablespoons fresh lime juice
- ¾ teaspoon coarse salt
- 1 tablespoon sweet paprika
- 1 tablespoon garam masala
- 1½ teaspoons ground black pepper

For the Stew:

- 2 pounds of salmon, cut into 2-inch pieces (largish, bite-sized pieces)
- Extra virgin olive oil, enough to coat the bottom of your pan *(Tip: 2 tablespoons is usually plenty.)*
- 2 medium onions, sliced thin
- 1 large bell pepper, seeded, de-stemmed and sliced thin
- 2 medium tomatoes, sliced thin
- Freshly ground black pepper, to taste
- 1 can (14 ounces) regular (not light) coconut milk
- 2 cups Swiss chard or fresh spinach
- Fresh cilantro, for garnish

KIDS CAN

- Wash and spin the chard
- Tear the leaves
- Smell spices for the marinade

WATCH OUT FOR

- Sharp knives
- Wash hands after handling raw fish

INSTRUCTIONS

1. In a large bowl, combine marinade ingredients and coat salmon. Cover and refrigerate for 30 minutes or longer if you have time.
2. In a large deep pot, heat oil. Add onions and sauté until translucent, about 3 minutes.
3. Add peppers, tomatoes and salmon. Add coconut milk. Cover the pot and simmer for 15 minutes.
4. Wash and spin the chard. Remove ribs and tear leaves into medium-sized pieces.
5. Stir and add in chard one handful at a time. Cook until chard reduces in size by half.
6. Serve with a garnish of cilantro.

TOM CATS

TOM CATS

Not last night, but the night before
Three tom cats came knocking at the door.
One with a trumpet, one with a drum,
And one with a pancake stuck on his bum.

I spent my childhood in New Orleans—the home of jazz cats and the origin of one of my all-time favorites: *the Muffuletta sandwich.*

It's a flat-as-a-pancake deli sandwich made on nine-inch round Italian bread filled with fresh olive salad. The real music behind a muffuletta is a delicious olive salad. Olive salad is made from ingredients you can find at the supermarket. And, not that its Louisiana roots need any improvement, but this recipe includes my personal "olive salad remix." Go ahead and play some jazz music like the Tom Cats in this rhyme and eat to the beat!

NUTRITION NIBBLE

If you want to raise a kid who eats just about everything, you should feed them what you eat—assuming you're eating a varied, healthy diet. After all, it's what cultures have done for most of human history. Olives are rich in healthy fats and packed with powerful antioxidants that protect your body from damaging molecules called free radicals. Olives, when pitted, are soft and easy for kids to eat. Each variety has a distinct flavor. If olives are new to your child, start with mild-flavored black olives.

MUFFULETTA SANDWICH

Makes: 1 sandwich or 12 wedges
Contains: Milk, Wheat, Tree Nuts

Challenge Level: Just a Pinch Involved
Active Time: 30 minutes
Total Time: 2 hours
(includes marinating and 1 hour resting time)

INGREDIENTS

For the Olive Salad:
- 1 cup sliced green olives, plus 1 tablespoon liquid from the jar
- 1 jar giardiniera, chopped
- 5 pickled cocktail onions, sliced
- 15 Kalamata olives, sliced and pitted
- 2 large pieces of roasted, marinated red bell pepper, diced
- 2 cloves garlic, minced
- ¼ cup pickle relish
- 1 teaspoon dried oregano
- 3 sprigs fresh parsley, leaves only, chopped
- 1 aji verde or peperoncino, seeded and sliced
- ¼ cup extra virgin olive oil

KIDS CAN
- Mix the ingredients of the olive salad
- Layer meats and cheeses
- Help wrap sandwich in plastic wrap

WATCH OUT FOR
- Sharp knives
- Impatience...this recipe takes a "long time" in a child's eyes.

For the Sandwich:
- 1 (9-inch round) Italian onion loaf cut in half (ciabatta works well here)
- 12 slices mozzarella
- 12 slices smoked provolone
- 12 slices salami
- 12 slices mortadella with Pistachios (can substitute with bologna)
- 12 slices low-sodium ham

INSTRUCTIONS

1. In a medium bowl combine all the ingredients for the olive salad. Cover with plastic wrap and let sit for 30 minutes so flavors combine.
2. Slice the big round bread loaf in half. If necessary, hollow out a little bit of the top and bottom.
3. Fill both sides of the bread with olive salad.
4. Alternate layers of all cheese and meats.
5. Close the sandwich and tightly wrap it with plastic wrap to hold all the juices in.
6. Let the sandwich rest for 1 hour or overnight.
7. Slice into wedges and serve cold or at room temperature.

LITTLE BLUE WHALE

LITTLE BLUE WHALE

The little blue whale with the little blue tail
With the blue tail. With the blue tail.
Can you see the blue whale in the big blue sea?
Swimming so merrily!

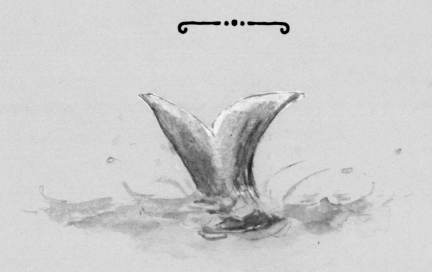

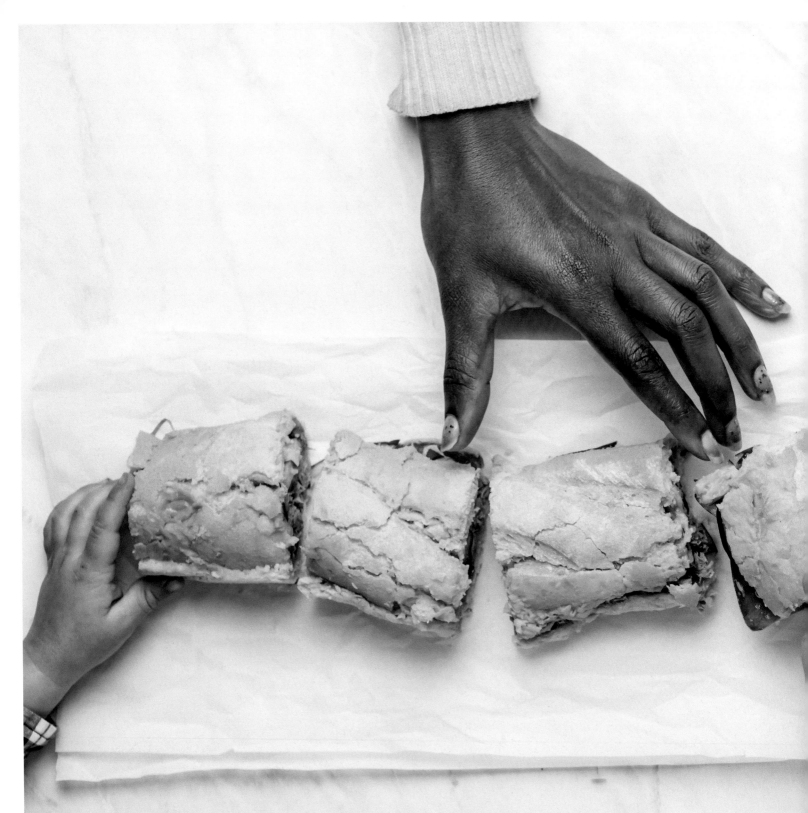

Pan Banget, "wet bread sandwich" or, as it's called in my house, "the sandwich you sit on," is a Mediterranean dish from the shores of Southern France. Though it sounds like a fancy "grown-up" food, my littles absolutely love it. Bathed in tangy niçoise cucumber dressing and piled high with tuna, tomatoes, fresh herbs and hard-boiled egg—it's as fun to eat as it is to make! Read on and make sure to include your kiddo in all the fun, tasty silliness of "the sandwich you sit on."

SIT ON IT TUNA NIÇOISE SANDWICH

NO WHALES WERE HARMED IN THE FLATTENING OF THE NIÇOISE SAMMY

NUTRITION NIBBLE   Inexpensive, high-quality protein and flavorful everyday vegetables make it easy to bring "The Mediterranean Diet" to your table. I often make this sandwich for the boys' lunch.

SIT ON IT TUNA NIÇOISE SANDWICH

Makes: 1 baguette or 8 mini sandwiches	**Challenge Level:** Piece of Cake
Contains: Wheat, Egg, Fish	**Active Time:** 30 minutes
Diet Type: Dairy Free	**Total Time:** 45 minutes (includes 15 minutes sitting time)

INGREDIENTS

For the Vinaigrette Dressing:

- ½ to 1 teaspoon anchovy paste, optional
- 2 garlic cloves, minced
- 2 teaspoons sherry vinegar (or other red vinegar)
- 2 teaspoons Dijon mustard
- Pinch of salt and freshly ground pepper
- 2 tablespoons extra virgin olive oil

For the Sandwich:

- ½ medium cucumber, seeds removed, sliced thin
- 1 medium ripe tomato, sliced thin
- ½ small red onion, sliced
- 1 baguette
- 10 to 12 ounces canned tuna, drained
- 8 large basil leaves
- 2 tablespoons sliced and pitted olives
- 1 hard-boiled egg, thinly sliced
- Baby lettuce leaves

KIDS CAN

- Pile on the veggies
- Sit on the sandwich
- Set the timer

WATCH OUT FOR

- Giggling, wiggling children having too much fun
- Juices leaking out of the plastic wrap (you may want to double wrap to protect clothes)

INSTRUCTIONS

1. Combine all vinaigrette ingredients in a jar and shake.
2. Add sliced cucumbers to vinaigrette and stir.
3. Soak sliced onion in cold water.
4. Cut the baguette in half horizontally. Pull out excess inner bread to make a "bed" for the fixings.
5. Spread half the dressed cucumbers on the bottom of the bread.
6. Drain the onions, and then top sandwich with tomato, lettuce and onion slices.
7. Pile on the tuna, basil, olives and egg slices.
8. Cover egg with remaining cucumbers and vinaigrette.
9. Place the other half of the bread on top and firmly press the sandwich together.
10. Wrap sandwich tightly in foil, waxed paper or plastic wrap, then place in a plastic bag.
11. Ready for the fun part? Have a child (or two) about 4 years old **sit on it** for 7 minutes on each side (or as long as you can get your child to sit still). If you don't have kids around, flatten with any heavy object.
12. Unwrap the sandwich, slice and serve.

PAT-A-CAKE

PAT-A-CAKE

Pat-a-cake, pat-a-cake, baker's man,
Bake me a cake as fast as you can.
Roll it and pat it and mark it with a "B"
And put it in the oven for Baby and me!

Pat-a-cake is the first nursery rhyme my boys learned by heart and a
great one for your littles because you can make it into a partner game.
Sit cross legged across from each other and clap hands together to the tune.
Then roll your hands and pat your knees. Expect lots of laughter and squeals
when you reach out to draw a "B" on their tummies. When you make this
recipe together, make sure to clap, roll, pat and of course, taste!

NUTRITION NIBBLE A balanced diet makes room for dessert. Restricting food (like sugar and treats) can backfire on parents. Kids need to learn how to incorporate sweets into their diet from you. Allowing these foods at home lets children know they don't need to sneak these desserts—they can be enjoyed in moderation as a family.

BEST EVER COCONUT CAKE

Makes: 1 cake or 16 slices
Contains: Wheat, Egg, Milk

Challenge Level: So Worth the Effort
Active Time: 1 hour
Total Time: 4 hours

Like most kids, my boys love cake, frosting and parties. I've got a whole other cookbook, *Celebrating with Mother Goose*, dedicated to desserts, snacks (which double as party food), and kid-friendly drinks to help your family eat well on special occasions—even if a special occasion with your family is just an ordinary night!

INGREDIENTS

For the Cake:

- 1 stick unsalted butter
- 3 tablespoons coconut oil
- ¾ cups granulated sugar
- 1½ tablespoons vanilla extract
- 3 eggs, room temperature
- 1¾ cups all-purpose flour
- 3 teaspoons baking powder
- ½ cup plain full-fat yogurt
- ¼ cup milk
- ½ teaspoon salt

For the Frosting:

- 1 packet (8 ounces) cream cheese, softened
- 1 stick unsalted butter, softened
- 1 tablespoon vanilla extract
- 4 to 5 cups powdered sugar
- Blackberries and blueberries to decorate

KIDS CAN

- Crack eggs with help
- Sift dry ingredients
- Prepare cake pans with cooking spray and parchment paper
- Wash berries and pat dry

WATCH OUT FOR

- Hot oven
- Cakes that are too warm or icing that is too cold make decorating impossible

INSTRUCTIONS ON NEXT PAGE

IF YOU THINK YOU HATE
COCONUT – THINK AGAIN!
YOU WILL LOVE THIS CAKE!

INSTRUCTIONS

For the Cake:

1. Preheat oven to 350°F, convection bake.
2. Cream butter, coconut oil and granulated sugar in your stand-up mixer using the whisk attachment.
3. Add eggs, one at a time, to the creamed butter and sugar. *(**Tip:** Give children a little bowl to crack their eggs into to avoid any shell pieces getting into the cake batter.)*
4. In a separate bowl, combine flour, baking powder and salt, then sift to remove any lumps. This improves the texture.
5. If using a stand-up mixer, change to paddle attachment and add sifted ingredients a little at a time until batter is smooth.
6. Pour batter into three or four 4-inch round, baking pans coated with cooking spray and lined on the bottom with parchment paper. Stop filling at the half-way mark to avoid a big mess in your oven. (**Note:** to make a two-tier cake like in the picture, use two different size cake pans and make a double batch of cake and icing. I find it is harder to frost a two-tier cake, so if this is your "first rodeo," maybe start with the one-tier cake.)
7. Bake 20 to 25 minutes or until each cake passes the "Toothpick Test." *(**Tip:** not all ovens heat evenly, so sometimes one cake pan is ready before the others. Be sure each pan passes the "Toothpick Test" before removing from the oven.)*
8. Cool cakes on a wire rack, then transfer to refrigerator. Allow to cool completely before decorating, about 2 hours.

BEST EVER COCONUT CAKE

INSTRUCTIONS

For the Vanilla Frosting:

9. Place softened butter and cream cheese in your stand-up mixer with the whisk attachment. Cream together until uniform in texture.

10. Add vanilla extract and continue to blend.

11. Sift powdered sugar and add a little at a time to the mixer. Be sure to scrape down the sides from time to time. (*Tip: I cover my stand-up mixer with a dish towel during this step to keep powdered sugar contained.*) Frosting will come together in 2 to 3 minutes.

12. Once all the powdered sugar is incorporated, taste. Add more vanilla or sugar as desired.

Assemble and Decorate the Cake:

13. Set cakes on the counter. Using a sharp bread knife, cut off the dome so you have 3 (or 4) flat-topped cakes. (*Tip: Bend down so you are eye level with the top of the cake in order to cut level horizontally.*)

14. Place a cake board on top of your turntable. (*Tip: A lazy Susan or cake turntable and a bench scraper make decorating easy-peasy!*)

15. Measure out 1½ cups of the **Vanilla Frosting** for the crumb coat. Leave the rest of the icing out so it's at room temperature for the final coat.

16. Take a big spoon of crumb coat icing and place it in the middle of the cake board. This will act like "glue" to hold down the cake.

17. Place the first cake layer on top of the icing.

18. Smear icing on top of the first layer of cake. Don't worry if it goes over the sides, you will scrape all the excess icing away later. Continue until you have all layers stacked, then smear any remaining icing on the sides.

19. Take a bench scraper and smooth all the overflow icing from the top of the cake onto the sides—this crumb coat captures cake crumbs so they don't show up in the outer, decorative icing layers. (*Tip: Set this "crumby" icing aside. You can mix it with the excess cake to make cake truffles. See my recipe in Celebrating with Mother Goose.*)

20. Put cake in the fridge for 10 minutes.

21. Decorate the outside with the remaining icing, blueberries and blackberries.

MOTHER GOOSE MIX UP — I've written this as a cake recipe, but it works just as well for cupcakes. Just reduce cooking time and simplify your decoration game.

Nutrient Analysis Index

Counting calories is not the focus of this book and I encourage you not to stress over that detail too much. Children need to eat to grow and develop healthily. And, when left to listen to their hunger cues, they're amazing self-regulators, eating more or less as they need. When the **Division of Responsbility** (for a refresher on what this is, see page 23) is respected and children can eat intuitively, diets tend to be balanced. With that said, here is the nutrition information for each recipe as a reference so that you can decide for yourself how to balance your family's eating.

CHAPTER 1: REFERENCE RECIPES

Chicken Stock (serving size: 1 cup)

Calories	Total Fat	Saturated Fat	Protein	Sodium	Carbs	Fiber	Sugars
90 kcals	3g	1g	6g	340mg	8g	0g	4g

Vegetable Broth (serving size: 1 cup)

Calories	Total Fat	Saturated Fat	Protein	Sodium	Carbs	Fiber	Sugars
20 kcals	0g	0g	1g	140mg	4g	1g	2g

Fish Stock (serving size: 1 cup)

Calories	Total Fat	Saturated Fat	Protein	Sodium	Carbs	Fiber	Sugars
40 kcals	2g	0g	5g	380mg	0g	0g	0g

Blow Wind Blow Gluten-Free Flour Blend (serving size: 3½ cups)

Calories	Total Fat	Saturated Fat	Protein	Sodium	Carbs	Fiber	Sugars
530 kcals	15g	4g	13g	55mg	89g	13g	3g

Presto Pesto (serving size: 2 tablespoons)

Calories	Total Fat	Saturated Fat	Protein	Sodium	Carbs	Fiber	Sugars
120 kcals	12g	2g	3g	65mg	1g	1g	0g

Nut Butter (serving size: 1 tablespoon)

Calories	Total Fat	Saturated Fat	Protein	Sodium	Carbs	Fiber	Sugars
120 kcals	11g	1.5g	4g	0mg	4g	2g	1g

Apple Butter (serving size: 2 tablespoons)

Calories	Total Fat	Saturated Fat	Protein	Sodium	Carbs	Fiber	Sugars
25 kcals	0g	0g	0g	0g	6g	0g	6g

Long-Grain White Rice (serving size: ½ cup)

Calories	Total Fat	Saturated Fat	Protein	Sodium	Carbs	Fiber	Sugars
100 kcals	0g	0g	2g	0g	23g	0g	0g

Basic Quinoa (serving size: ½ cup)

Calories	Total Fat	Saturated Fat	Protein	Sodium	Carbs	Fiber	Sugars
136 kcals	4g	0g	4g	170mg	19g	2g	0g

Whole Grain (Brown) Rice (serving size: ½ cup)

Calories	Total Fat	Saturated Fat	Protein	Sodium	Carbs	Fiber	Sugars
125 kcals	1g	0g	3g	4mg	26g	2g	0g

Classic Couscous (serving size: ½ cup) *assumes cooked with stock

Calories	Total Fat	Saturated Fat	Protein	Sodium	Carbs	Fiber	Sugars
84 kcals	0g	0g	3g	150mg	18g	1g	0g

NUTRIENT ANALYSIS INDEX

Basic Bulgur (serving size: ½ cup)

Calories	Total Fat	Saturated Fat	Protein	Sodium	Carbs	Fiber	Sugars
76 kcals	3g	0g	3g	165g	14g	3g	0g

Basic Hulled Barley (serving size: ½ cup)

Calories	Total Fat	Saturated Fat	Protein	Sodium	Carbs	Fiber	Sugars
100 kcals	0g	0g	1g	2mg	25g	3g	0g

Pasta (serving size: ½ cup)

Calories	Total Fat	Saturated Fat	Protein	Sodium	Carbs	Fiber	Sugars
100 kcals	0.5g	0g	4g	15mg	21g	1g	1g

Zoodles (serving size: 1 cup)

Calories	Total Fat	Saturated Fat	Protein	Sodium	Carbs	Fiber	Sugars
26 kcals	1.5g	0g	1g	0mg	2g	1g	0g

CHAPTER 2: GOOD MORNING

Chinese Egg Cake Muffins (serving size: 1 muffin)

Calories	Total Fat	Saturated Fat	Protein	Sodium	Carbs	Fiber	Sugars
40 kcals	2g	0g	1g	10mg	5g	0g	3g

Two-Bite Blueberry Muffins (serving size: 1 muffin)

Calories	Total Fat	Saturated Fat	Protein	Sodium	Carbs	Fiber	Sugars
110 kcals	5g	3g	1g	105mg	18g	1g	8g

NUTRIENT ANALYSIS INDEX

Banana Granola Muffin Cups (serving size: 1 filled granola muffin cup)

Calories	Total Fat	Saturated Fat	Protein	Sodium	Carbs	Fiber	Sugars
140 kcals	5g	0.5g	4g	35mg	19g	2g	8g

Princess Granola (serving size: ⅓ cup)

Calories	Total Fat	Saturated Fat	Protein	Sodium	Carbs	Fiber	Sugars
230 kcals	16g	6g	5g	30mg	22g	4g	10g

Papaya Boats (serving size: ½ boat)

Calories	Total Fat	Saturated Fat	Protein	Sodium	Carbs	Fiber	Sugars
290g	14g	8g	7g	25mg	38g	5g	25g

Spirulina Smoothie Bowl (serving size: 4 ounces)

Calories	Total Fat	Saturated Fat	Protein	Sodium	Carbs	Fiber	Sugars
90 kcals	2g	0.5g	4g	45mg	14g	2g	11g

Plum Porridge (serving size: ¼ cup plus plums)

Calories	Total Fat	Saturated Fat	Protein	Sodium	Carbs	Fiber	Sugars
110 kcals	2g	0g	3g	80mg	20g	2g	5g

Carrot Cake Overnight Oats (serving size: ½ cup)

Calories	Total Fat	Saturated Fat	Protein	Sodium	Carbs	Fiber	Sugars
200 kcals	9g	4g	6g	170mg	24g	4g	13g

Sky-High Mushroom Quiche (serving size: 1 slice)

Calories	Total Fat	Saturated Fat	Protein	Sodium	Carbs	Fiber	Sugars
450 kcals	35g	18g	13g	390mg	23g	1g	4g

NUTRIENT ANALYSIS INDEX

Weekday Scrambled Eggs (serving size: 1 scrambled egg) **Note**: *nutrient analysis includes cream cheese*

Calories	Total Fat	Saturated Fat	Protein	Sodium	Carbs	Fiber	Sugars
100 kcals	8g	3.5g	6g	75mg	1g	0g	0g

Weekend Baked Eggs (serving size: 1 cocotte)

Calories	Total Fat	Saturated Fat	Protein	Sodium	Carbs	Fiber	Sugars
100 kcals	6g	2.5g	7g	230mg	3g	1g	1g

Aji Amarillo Sauce (serving size ¼ cup)

Calories	Total Fat	Saturated Fat	Protein	Sodium	Carbs	Fiber	Sugars
70 kcals	4.5g	2g	1g	350mg	8g	2g	2g

Chocolate Mystery Bread and Muffins (serving size: 1 slice bread or 1 muffin)

Calories	Total Fat	Saturated Fat	Protein	Sodium	Carbs	Fiber	Sugars
210 kcals	12g	3g	4g	100g	23g	2g	13g

Silver Spoonbread (serving size: ½ cup)

Calories	Total Fat	Saturated Fat	Protein	Sodium	Carbs	Fiber	Sugars
130 kcals	8g	4.5g	5g	150mg	10g	0g	4g

Heart Tarts (serving size: 1 tart)

Calories	Total Fat	Saturated Fat	Protein	Sodium	Carbs	Fiber	Sugars
390 kcals	16g	10g	4g	240mg	29g	3g	29g

Braided Egg Buns (serving size: 1 bun)

Calories	Total Fat	Saturated Fat	Protein	Sodium	Carbs	Fiber	Sugars
270 kcals	9g	1g	7g	250mg	42g	2g	3g

Cake Donuts with Mulberry Glaze (serving size: 1 donut)

Calories	Total Fat	Saturated Fat	Protein	Sodium	Carbs	Fiber	Sugars
140 kcals	8g	2g	2g	65mg	17g	1g	10g

Yogurt Plumcake with Plum Glaze (serving size: 1 slice)

Calories	Total Fat	Saturated Fat	Protein	Sodium	Carbs	Fiber	Sugars
370 kcals	15g	4g	5g	130mg	58g	2g	42g

Puppy Dog Tails (serving size: 1 tail)

Note: Recipe analysis assumes 2 tablespoons each of ground cinnamon, chocolate sprinkles and sweetened coconut flakes for the garnish.

Calories	Total Fat	Saturated Fat	Protein	Sodium	Carbs	Fiber	Sugars
140 kcals	6g	1g	2g	35mg	19g	3g	12g

Cinnamon Rolls (serving size: 1 roll)

Note: analysis is for cinnamon rolls without icing.

Calories	Total Fat	Saturated Fat	Protein	Sodium	Carbs	Fiber	Sugars
290 kcals	6g	3.5g	6g	310mg	53g	2g	19g

CHAPTER 3: SLURPY SOUPS

Seafood Soup (serving size: 1 cup)

Calories	Total Fat	Saturated Fat	Protein	Sodium	Carbs	Fiber	Sugars
210kcals	8g	1g	19g	470mg	9g	1g	2g

Team Chicken Soup (serving size: 1 cup)

Calories	Total Fat	Saturated Fat	Protein	Sodium	Carbs	Fiber	Sugars
260 kcals	13g	4.5g	16g	670mg	21g	3g	8g

NUTRIENT ANALYSIS INDEX

Egg Drop Soup (serving size: 1 cup)

Calories	Total Fat	Saturated Fat	Protein	Sodium	Carbs	Fiber	Sugars
180 kcals	10g	4g	12g	400mg	10g	0g	4g

Lentil Stew (serving size: ½ cup)

Calories	Total Fat	Saturated Fat	Protein	Sodium	Carbs	Fiber	Sugars
140 kcals	0g	0g	9g	220mg	25g	6g	7g

Pea, Prosciutto and Mint Risotto (serving size: ½ cup)

Calories	Total Fat	Saturated Fat	Protein	Sodium	Carbs	Fiber	Sugars
130 kcals	4.5g	2g	5g	310mg	18g	2g	2g

Pea and Avocado Gazpacho (serving size: 1 cup)

Calories	Total Fat	Saturated Fat	Protein	Sodium	Carbs	Fiber	Sugars
210 kcals	14g	2g	6g	260mg	19g	10g	5g

Porotos Con Pilco (serving size: 1 cup)

Calories	Total Fat	Saturated Fat	Protein	Sodium	Carbs	Fiber	Sugars
110 kcals	2g	0g	3g	85mg	20g	5g	7g

CHAPTER 4: PASTA AND GRAINS

Runaway Meatballs (serving size: 1 meatball)

Calories	Total Fat	Saturated Fat	Protein	Sodium	Carbs	Fiber	Sugars
50 kcals	3.5g	1.5g	4g	15mg	1g	0g	0g

Rich Red Sauce (serving size: 1 cup)

Calories	Total Fat	Saturated Fat	Protein	Sodium	Carbs	Fiber	Sugars
110 kcals	5g	0.5g	3g	160mg	15g	4g	8g

Black and White Pasta Alfredo (serving size: ½ cup)

Calories	Total Fat	Saturated Fat	Protein	Sodium	Carbs	Fiber	Sugars
225 kcals	23g	15g	11g	300mg	8g	1g	1.5g

Ratatouille Lasagna (serving size: 4 ounce piece)

Calories	Total Fat	Saturated Fat	Protein	Sodium	Carbs	Fiber	Sugars
330 kcals	12g	4.5g	16g	480mg	40g	3g	10g

Fig and Quinoa Salad (serving size: ½ cup)

Calories	Total Fat	Saturated Fat	Protein	Sodium	Carbs	Fiber	Sugars
260 kcals	15g	4.5g	8g	210mg	25g	5g	4g

Avocado Tabbouleh (serving size: ½ cup)

Calories	Total Fat	Saturated Fat	Protein	Sodium	Carbs	Fiber	Sugars
210 kcals	12g	1.5g	5g	45mg	23g	7g	2g

Grilled Peach Couscous (serving size: ½ cup)

Calories	Total Fat	Saturated Fat	Protein	Sodium	Carbs	Fiber	Sugars
200 kcals	15g	4g	4g	160mg	14g	2g	7g

Southwest Rice Salad (serving size: ½ cup)

Calories	Total Fat	Saturated Fat	Protein	Sodium	Carbs	Fiber	Sugars
230 kcals	9g	1.5g	7g	80mg	31g	5g	5g

NUTRIENT ANALYSIS INDEX

CHAPTER 5: TASTY VEGGIES

One Ingredient Portobello Mushroom Steaks (serving size: 1 mushroom or 3 ounces)

Calories	Total Fat	Saturated Fat	Protein	Sodium	Carbs	Fiber	Sugars
30 kcals	0g	0g	3g	10mg	4g	2g	2g

Two Ingredient Paneer (serving size: 1 ounce)

Calories	Total Fat	Saturated Fat	Protein	Sodium	Carbs	Fiber	Sugars
100 kcals	5g	3g	5g	85mg	8g	0g	8g

Three Ingredient Zucchini Fingers (serving size: 4 fingers)

Calories	Total Fat	Saturated Fat	Protein	Sodium	Carbs	Fiber	Sugars
90 kcals	2g	0.5g	5g	80mg	13g	2g	3g

Four Ingredient Cauliflower Tacos (serving size: ½ cup)

Calories	Total Fat	Saturated Fat	Protein	Sodium	Carbs	Fiber	Sugars
50 kcals	2g	0g	2g	190mg	7g	2g	2g

Five Ingredient Beet Burgers: (serving size: 1 patty)

Calories	Total Fat	Saturated Fat	Protein	Sodium	Carbs	Fiber	Sugars
180 kcals	1g	0g	8g	350mg	36g	6g	4g

Black Bean and Artichoke Enchilada Wreath (serving size: 1 cone)

Calories	Total Fat	Saturated Fat	Protein	Sodium	Carbs	Fiber	Sugars
180 kcals	5g	2.5g	6g	210mg	26g	3g	1g

Enchilada Sauce (serving size: 1 tablespoon)

Calories	Total Fat	Saturated Fat	Protein	Sodium	Carbs	Fiber	Sugars
15 kcals	1.5g	0g	0	35mg	1g	0g	0g

Veggie Stir Fry (serving size: 1 cup)

Calories	Total Fat	Saturated Fat	Protein	Sodium	Carbs	Fiber	Sugars
70 kcals	3.5g	0g	3g	330mg	9g	2g	4g

Honey-Spiced Roasted Pumpkin (serving size: 4 ounces)

Calories	Total Fat	Saturated Fat	Protein	Sodium	Carbs	Fiber	Sugars
270 kcals	15g	6g	8g	30mg	28g	1g	23g

Sweet Potato Fried Rice (serving size: ½ cup)

Calories	Total Fat	Saturated Fat	Protein	Sodium	Carbs	Fiber	Sugars
130 kcals	7g	1g	5g	340mg	13g	3g	4g

Roasted Brussels Sprouts and Potatoes (serving size: ½ cup)

Calories	Total Fat	Saturated Fat	Protein	Sodium	Carbs	Fiber	Sugars
120 kcals	5g	0.5g	2g	250mg	18g	3g	3g

Potato Soup (serving size: 1 cup)

Calories	Total Fat	Saturated Fat	Protein	Sodium	Carbs	Fiber	Sugars
70 kcals	4g	2g	2g	30mg	8g	1g	2g

Truffle Fries (serving size: ½ cup or 2 kid-sized handfuls)

Calories	Total Fat	Saturated Fat	Protein	Sodium	Carbs	Fiber	Sugars
260 kcals	16g	3g	5g	480mg	27g	3g	1g

NUTRIENT ANALYSIS INDEX

Romesco (serving size: ½ cup)

Calories	Total Fat	Saturated Fat	Protein	Sodium	Carbs	Fiber	Sugars
190 kcals	19g	2.5g	2g	30mg	6g	2g	3g

Honey Peas (serving size: ⅓ cup)

Calories	Total Fat	Saturated Fat	Protein	Sodium	Carbs	Fiber	Sugars
100 kcals	5g	1.5g	3g	0mg	10g	3g	5g

Thai Cucumber Salad (serving size: 1cup)

Calories	Total Fat	Saturated Fat	Protein	Sodium	Carbs	Fiber	Sugars
120 kcals	10g	1.5g	4g	75mg	8g	2g	3g

Celery Slaw (serving size: 1 cup)

Calories	Total Fat	Saturated Fat	Protein	Sodium	Carbs	Fiber	Sugars
80 kcals	5g	0.5g	1g	210mg	8g	2g	6g

King Cole's Slaw (serving size: ½ cup)

Calories	Total Fat	Saturated Fat	Protein	Sodium	Carbs	Fiber	Sugars
100 kcals	7g	1g	1g	360mg	10g	2g	8g

Easy Cream Spinach (serving size: ¼ cup)

Calories	Total Fat	Saturated Fat	Protein	Sodium	Carbs	Fiber	Sugars
170 kcals	15g	9g	5g	220mg	5g	2g	1g

Blueberry Corn Salad (serving size: ¼ cup)

Calories	Total Fat	Saturated Fat	Protein	Sodium	Carbs	Fiber	Sugars
130 kcals	7g	1.5g	3g	250mg	16g	2g	10g

Mango Pomegranate Salad (serving size: ½ cup)

Calories	Total Fat	Saturated Fat	Protein	Sodium	Carbs	Fiber	Sugars
150 kcals	10g	3g	3g	410mg	14g	2g	12g

CHAPTER 6: ALL THE MEATS

King's Meat Pie (serving size: 1 slice)   ***Note:*** *nutrient analysis assumes 90% lean ground beef (10% fat)*

Calories	Total Fat	Saturated Fat	Protein	Sodium	Carbs	Fiber	Sugars
430 kcals	26g	11g	19g	360mg	29g	2g	7g

Salt and Vinegar Steak (serving size: 4 ounces)

Calories	Total Fat	Saturated Fat	Protein	Sodium	Carbs	Fiber	Sugars
230 kcals	18g	5g	16g	590mg	1g	0g	1g

Almond Cauliflower Purée (serving size: ½ cup)

Calories	Total Fat	Saturated Fat	Protein	Sodium	Carbs	Fiber	Sugars
220 kcals	20g	9g	5g	70mg	9g	5g	3g

Tom's Pulled Pork (serving size: 4 ounce)

Calories	Total Fat	Saturated Fat	Protein	Sodium	Carbs	Fiber	Sugars
220 kcals	13g	4g	19g	210mg	6g	0g	3g

Sweet and Sour Drumsticks (serving size: 1 drumstick)

Calories	Total Fat	Saturated Fat	Protein	Sodium	Carbs	Fiber	Sugars
290 kcals	14g	3.5g	25g	530mg	14g	0g	12g

NUTRIENT ANALYSIS INDEX

Chicken and Dumplings (serving size: ½ cup)

Calories	Total Fat	Saturated Fat	Protein	Sodium	Carbs	Fiber	Sugars
210 kcals	7g	4.5g	15g	500mg	22g	2g	4g

Chicken and Plum Skillet (serving size: 4 ounces)

Calories	Total Fat	Saturated Fat	Protein	Sodium	Carbs	Fiber	Sugars
160 kcals	4.5g	1.5g	19g	250mg	10g	1g	5g

Jamaican Jerk Chicken Wings (serving size: 2 wings)

Calories	Total Fat	Saturated Fat	Protein	Sodium	Carbs	Fiber	Sugars
150 kcals	4.5g	1g	15g	680mg	14g	2g	7g

Steamed Artichoke with Vinaigrette (serving size: 1 artichoke and 2 tablespoons vinaigrette)

Calories	Total Fat	Saturated Fat	Protein	Sodium	Carbs	Fiber	Sugars
190 kcals	14g	2g	3g	100mg	14g	10g	4g

Teriyaki Steak Skillet (serving size: 3 ounces)

Calories	Total Fat	Saturated Fat	Protein	Sodium	Carbs	Fiber	Sugars
160 kcals	5g	2g	21g	925mg	7g	1g	5g

Spaghetti Squash Shrimp Pad Thai (serving size: 1 cup)

Calories	Total Fat	Saturated Fat	Protein	Sodium	Carbs	Fiber	Sugars
270 kcals	13g	2.5g	22g	330mg	21g	2g	13g

Teriyaki Salmon (serving size: 5 ounces)

Calories	Total Fat	Saturated Fat	Protein	Sodium	Carbs	Fiber	Sugars
220 kcals	12g	2.5g	24g	740mg	4g	0g	3g

Mahi Mahi Bowtie Pasta (serving size: 4 ounces)

Calories	Total Fat	Saturated Fat	Protein	Sodium	Carbs	Fiber	Sugars
400 kcals	8g	1g	23g	75mg	61g	5g	4g

Crispy Coconut Tilapia (serving size: 4 ounces)

Calories	Total Fat	Saturated Fat	Protein	Sodium	Carbs	Fiber	Sugars
180 kcals	4.5g	2.5g	20g	200mg	15g	1g	3g

Piña and Avocado Salsa (serving size: 4 tablespoons)

Calories	Total Fat	Saturated Fat	Protein	Sodium	Carbs	Fiber	Sugars
90 kcals	5g	0.5g	1g	5mg	12g	3g	7g

Moqueca Stew with Salmon (serving size: 1 cup)

Calories	Total Fat	Saturated Fat	Protein	Sodium	Carbs	Fiber	Sugars
360 kcals	26g	13g	25g	290mg	8g	2g	3g

Muffuletta Sandwich (serving size: 1 wedge)

Calories	Total Fat	Saturated Fat	Protein	Sodium	Carbs	Fiber	Sugars
450 kcals	31g	12g	32g	1930mg	10g	1g	1g

Sit On It Tuna Niçoise Sandwich (serving size: 1 piece)

Calories	Total Fat	Saturated Fat	Protein	Sodium	Carbs	Fiber	Sugars
120 kcals	4g	1g	13g	240mg	8g	1g	1g

BONUS RECIPE: Best Ever Coconut Cake (serving size: 1 slice)

Calories	Total Fat	Saturated Fat	Protein	Sodium	Carbs	Fiber	Sugars
420 kcals	20g	13g	4g	250mg	57g	1g	45g

Fresh Ingredient Index

It bums me out when fresh ingredients go to waste, so I designed this index to help maximize ingredients that have a shorter shelf life. You won't find the longer-lasting ingredients like butter, ghee, extra virgin olive oil, mayonnaise, onion, garlic or canned and dried goods here. These items are less likely to end up in the bin due to spoilage. But fruits, vegetables, some dairy, chicken, fish and meat are listed in this index for your quick reference.

Most cookbook indexes will list the recipes in ABC order and give the page number where they appear. My index is a little bit different. This index is organized alphabetically by fresh ingredient and then by order of appearance in the book.

WHY?

Because I often open the fridge to see ingredients I need to use up before they rot and then search for a recipe. So when you have a "Whoops!, berries are getting mushy" moment you can find a recipe that will come to the rescue. **Note:** You can make **Heart Tarts** (p. 153) or **Two-Bite Blueberry Muffins** (p. 107).

Use this Fresh Ingredient Index...

⟨TO⟩ MAXIMIZE INGREDIENTS

If, for example, you make Chicken and Plum Skillet and you have some plums left over, you can look up plums under "P" in the index. You'll find the other recipes that use plums as an ingredient (Plum Porridge, Yogurt Plumcake with Plum Glaze) so you can make those with any leftover fruit you may have. If your lemon tree is full of fresh, ripe fruit, turn to "L" in the index to see how to put all your lemons to good use.

⟨TO⟩ STRETCH YOUR FOOD BUDGET

You can also use this index as a meal planner. Look up recipes that have a fresh ingredient you see on sale at the grocery store (Avocados! Salmon!) to maximize your food budget. For maximum savings, skip convenience products like precut fruit and veg as you pay more for work that's done for you.

⟨TO⟩ SATISFY A CRAVING

Craving a particular food? If it's a fresh ingredient, look it up in the index to see what you can make to satisfy that craving!

MY TOP TIPS FOR MAXIMIZING YOUR PRODUCE:

 Make stock or soup with veggies that have passed their prime. Find some overripe fruit? Blitz up a smoothie, or freeze in popsicle molds for a fresh fruit pop.

 Overly ripe bananas add some natural sweetness when added to baked goods (like **Chocolate Mystery Bread** on page 143).

 Save stalks: peel the tough outer layers from the stems of cauliflower and broccoli then grate them into salads (like **King Cole's Slaw** on page 293) or sauté, roast or steam them just as you would the florets.

 Ugly produce is usually just as tasty as its pretty counterparts. Show ugly fruits and veggies some love and less will end up in the supermarket and farm waste bins. My kids and I make a game of finding the ugliest tomato, avocado or squash (for example) in the supermarket to put in our carts.

 Keep salad combos seasonal by using what naturally grows at the same time, like **Blueberry Corn Salad** on page 301.

LACEY J. MAURITZ, RDN • AUTHOR

Lacey is a food-loving, registered dietitian, wife and mom who is ultra-passionate about child and family nutrition. Her goal is to engage parents and their little ones in the process of preparing, cooking and—the best part—eating meals. This is her third cookbook.

Lacey lives in Jacksonville, Florida, and when away from her kitchen, enjoys spending time with her family, playing tennis, and traveling.

For more information, please visit www.storybooknutrition.com

© 2020 Storybook Nutrition, LLC
Printed in Canada
ISBN 978-1-7349520-0-1 (print) / 978-1-7349520-1-8 (digital)

All rights reserved. No part of this publication may be reproduced, stored in a retrieval system or transmitted, in any form or by any means, electronic, mechanical, photocopying, recording or otherwise, without the prior permission of Storybook Nutrition, LLC.

Author: Lacey J. Mauritz, RDN
Illustrator: Jacqueline Taylor
Designer: Stockton Eller
Food Photography: Lorena Salinas
Cover Photography: Sarah Eddy
Editor: Sarah Zerkel